PENGU

Founding

Genera

Supervisory Editors.

T. J. B. SPENCER, ... Director of the Shake-speare Institute of the University of Birmingham, was the founding editor of the New Penguin Shakespeare, for which he edited both *Romeo and Juliet* and *Hamlet*.

STANLEY WELLS is Emeritus Professor of the University of Birmingham and Chairman of the Shakespeare Birthplace Trust. He is general editor of the Oxford Shakespeare and his books include *Shakespeare: The Poet and His Plays*, *Shakespeare: For All Time*, *Looking for Sex in Shakespeare* and (with Paul Edmondson) *Shakespeare's Sonnets*.

R. A. FOAKES is Emeritus Professor of English at the University of California, Los Angeles. His recent books include *Shakespeare and Violence* and an edition of *Henslowe's Diary*.

JANETTE DILLON is Professor of Drama at the University of Nottingham. She has published widely on Shakespeare and Renaissance drama, and her recent publications include *Language and Stage in Medieval and Renaissance England*, *Theatre, Court and City 1595–1610: Drama and Social Space in London* and *Performance and Spectacle in Hall's Chronicle*.

IN SHAKESPEARE

William Shakespeare

MUCH ADO ABOUT NOTHING

Edited with a Commentary by R. A. Foakes
Introduced by Janette Dillon

PENGUIN BOOKS

PENGUIN BOOKS

Published by the Penguin Group
Penguin Books Ltd, 80 Strand, London WC2R ORL, England
Penguin Group (USA) Inc., 375 Hudson Street, New York, New York 10014, USA
Penguin Group (Canada), 10 Alcorn Avenue, Toronto, Ontario, Canada M4V 3B2
(a division of Pearson Penguin Canada Inc.)
Penguin Ireland, 25 St Stephen's Green, Dublin 2, Ireland (a division of Penguin Books Ltd)
Penguin Group (Australia), 250 Camberwell Road, Camberwell, Victoria 3124, Australia
(a division of Pearson Australia Group Pty Ltd)
Penguin Books India Pvt Ltd, 11 Community Centre, Panchsheel Park, New Delhi – 110 017, India
Penguin Group (NZ), cnr Airborne and Rosedale Roads, Albany, Auckland 1310, New Zealand
(a division of Pearson New Zealand Ltd)
Penguin Books (South Africa) (Pty) Ltd, 24 Sturdee Avenue, Rosebank 2196, South Africa

Penguin Books Ltd, Registered Offices: 80 Strand, London WC2R ORL, England

www.penguin.com

This edition first published in Penguin Books 1968
Reissued in the Penguin Shakespeare series 2005

14

This edition copyright © Penguin Books, 1968, 1996
Account of the Text and Commentary copyright © R. A. Foakes, 1968
General Introduction and Chronology copyright © Stanley Wells, 2005
Introduction, The Play in Performance and Further Reading copyright © Janette Dillon, 2005

All rights reserved

The moral right of the editors has been asserted

Set in 11.5/12.5 PostScript Monotype Fournier
Typeset by Palimpsest Book Production Limited, Polmont, Stirlingshire
Printed in England by Clays Ltd, St Ives plc

Except in the United States of America, this book is sold subject
to the condition that it shall not, by way of trade or otherwise, be lent,
re-sold, hired out, or otherwise circulated without the publisher's
prior consent in any form of binding or cover other than that in
which it is published and without a similar condition including this
condition being imposed on the subsequent purchaser

ISBN-13: 978-0-141-01230-8

www.greenpenguin.co.uk

Penguin Books is committed to a sustainable
future for our business, our readers and our
planet. This book is made from paper certified
by the Forest Stewardship Council.

Contents

General Introduction

Every play by Shakespeare is unique. This is part of his greatness. A restless and indefatigable experimenter, he moved with a rare amalgamation of artistic integrity and dedicated professionalism from one kind of drama to another. Never shackled by convention, he offered his actors the alternation between serious and comic modes from play to play, and often also within the plays themselves, that the repertory system within which he worked demanded, and which provided an invaluable stimulus to his imagination. Introductions to individual works in this series attempt to define their individuality. But there are common factors that underpin Shakespeare's career.

Nothing in his heredity offers clues to the origins of his genius. His upbringing in Stratford-upon-Avon, where he was born in 1564, was unexceptional. His mother, born Mary Arden, came from a prosperous farming family. Her father chose her as his executor over her eight sisters and his four stepchildren when she was only in her late teens, which suggests that she was of more than average practical ability. Her husband John, a glover, apparently unable to write, was nevertheless a capable businessman and loyal townsfellow, who seems to have fallen on relatively hard times in later life. He would have been brought up as a Catholic, and may have retained

Catholic sympathies, but his son subscribed publicly to Anglicanism throughout his life.

The most important formative influence on Shakespeare was his school. As the son of an alderman who became bailiff (or mayor) in 1568, he had the right to attend the town's grammar school. Here he would have received an education grounded in classical rhetoric and oratory, studying authors such as Ovid, Cicero and Quintilian, and would have been required to read, speak, write and even think in Latin from his early years. This classical education permeates Shakespeare's work from the beginning to the end of his career. It is apparent in the self-conscious classicism of plays of the early 1590s such as the tragedy of *Titus Andronicus*, *The Comedy of Errors*, and the narrative poems *Venus and Adonis* (1592–3) and *The Rape of Lucrece* (1593–4), and is still evident in his latest plays, informing the dream visions of *Pericles* and *Cymbeline* and the masque in *The Tempest*, written between 1607 and 1611. It inflects his literary style throughout his career. In his earliest writings the verse, based on the ten-syllabled, five-beat iambic pentameter, is highly patterned. Rhetorical devices deriving from classical literature, such as alliteration and antithesis, extended similes and elaborate wordplay, abound. Often, as in *Love's Labour's Lost* and *A Midsummer Night's Dream*, he uses rhyming patterns associated with lyric poetry, each line self-contained in sense, the prose as well as the verse employing elaborate figures of speech. Writing at a time of linguistic ferment, Shakespeare frequently imports Latinisms into English, coining words such as abstemious, addiction, incarnadine and adjunct. He was also heavily influenced by the eloquent translations of the Bible in both the Bishops' and the Geneva versions. As his experience grows, his verse and prose become more supple, the patterning less apparent, more ready to accommodate the rhythms of ordinary speech, more colloquial in diction, as in the speeches of the Nurse in *Romeo and Juliet*, the characterful prose of Falstaff and Hamlet's soliloquies. The effect is of increasing psychological realism, reaching its greatest heights in *Hamlet*, *Othello*, *King Lear*, *Macbeth* and *Antony and Cleopatra*. Gradually he discovered ways of adapting the regular beat of the pentameter to make it an infinitely flexible instrument for matching thought with feeling. Towards the end of his career, in plays such as *The Winter's Tale*, *Cymbeline* and *The Tempest*, he adopts a more highly mannered style, in keeping with the more overtly symbolical and emblematical mode in which he is writing.

So far as we know, Shakespeare lived in Stratford till after his marriage to Anne Hathaway, eight years his senior, in 1582. They had three children: a daughter, Susanna, born in 1583 within six months of their marriage, and twins, Hamnet and Judith, born in 1585. The next seven years of Shakespeare's life are virtually a blank. Theories that he may have been, for instance, a schoolmaster, or a lawyer, or a soldier, or a sailor, lack evidence to support them. The first reference to him in print, in Robert Greene's pamphlet *Greene's Groatsworth of Wit* of 1592, parodies a line from *Henry VI, Part III*, implying that Shakespeare was already an established playwright. It seems likely that at some unknown point after the birth of his twins he joined a theatre company and gained experience as both actor and writer in the provinces and London. The London theatres closed because of plague in 1593 and 1594; and during these years, perhaps recognizing the need for an alternative career, he wrote and published the narrative poems *Venus and Adonis* and *The Rape of Lucrece*. These are the only works we can be certain that Shakespeare himself was responsible for putting into print. Each bears the author's dedication to Henry Wriothesley, Earl of Southampton (1573–1624), the second in warmer terms than the first. Southampton, younger than Shakespeare by ten years, is the only person to whom he personally dedicated works. The Earl may have been a close friend, perhaps even the beautiful and adored young man whom Shakespeare celebrates in his *Sonnets*.

The resumption of playing after the plague years saw the founding of the Lord Chamberlain's Men, a company to which Shakespeare was to belong for the rest of his career, as actor, shareholder and playwright. No other dramatist of the period had so stable a relationship with a single company. Shakespeare knew the actors for whom he was writing and the conditions in which they performed. The permanent company was made up of around twelve to fourteen players, but one actor often played more than one role in a play and additional actors were hired as needed. Led by the tragedian Richard Burbage (1568–1619) and, initially, the comic actor Will Kemp (d. 1603), they rapidly achieved a high reputation, and when King James I succeeded Queen Elizabeth I in 1603 they were renamed as the King's Men. All the women's parts were played by boys; there is no evidence that any female role was ever played by a male actor over the age of about eighteen. Shakespeare had enough confidence in his boys to write for them long and demanding roles such as Rosalind (who, like other heroines of the romantic comedies, is disguised as a boy for much of the action) in *As You Like It*, Lady Macbeth and Cleopatra. But there are far more fathers than mothers, sons than daughters, in his plays, few if any of which require more than the company's normal complement of three or four boys.

The company played primarily in London's public playhouses – there were almost none that we know of in the rest of the country – initially in the Theatre, built in Shoreditch in 1576, and from 1599 in the Globe, on Bankside. These were wooden, more or less circular structures, open to the air, with a thrust stage surmounted by a canopy and jutting into the area where spectators who paid one penny stood, and surrounded by galleries where it was possible to be seated on payment of an additional penny. Though properties such as cauldrons, stocks, artificial trees or beds could indicate locality, there was no representational scenery. Sound effects such as flourishes of trumpets, music both martial and amorous, and accompaniments to songs were provided by the company's musicians. Actors entered through doors in the back wall of the stage. Above it was a balconied area that could represent the walls of a town (as in *King John*), or a castle (as in *Richard II*), and indeed a balcony (as in *Romeo and Juliet*). In 1609 the company also acquired the use of the Blackfriars, a smaller, indoor theatre to which admission was more expensive, and which permitted the use of more spectacular stage effects such as the descent of Jupiter on an eagle in *Cymbeline* and of goddesses in *The Tempest*. And they would frequently perform before the court in royal residences and, on their regular tours into the provinces, in non-theatrical spaces such as inns, guildhalls and the great halls of country houses.

Early in his career Shakespeare may have worked in collaboration, perhaps with Thomas Nashe (1567–c. 1601) in *Henry VI, Part I* and with George Peele (1556–96) in *Titus Andronicus*. And towards the end he collaborated with George Wilkins (*fl.* 1604–8) in *Pericles*, and with his younger colleagues Thomas Middleton (1580–1627), in *Timon of Athens*, and John Fletcher (1579–1625), in *Henry*

VIII, *The Two Noble Kinsmen* and the lost play *Cardenio*. Shakespeare's output dwindled in his last years, and he died in 1616 in Stratford, where he owned a fine house, New Place, and much land. His only son had died at the age of eleven, in 1596, and his last descendant died in 1670. New Place was destroyed in the eighteenth century but the other Stratford houses associated with his life are maintained and displayed to the public by the Shakespeare Birthplace Trust.

One of the most remarkable features of Shakespeare's plays is their intellectual and emotional scope. They span a great range from the lightest of comedies, such as *The Two Gentlemen of Verona* and *The Comedy of Errors*, to the profoundest of tragedies, such as *King Lear* and *Macbeth*. He maintained an output of around two plays a year, ringing the changes between comic and serious. All his comedies have serious elements: Shylock, in *The Merchant of Venice*, almost reaches tragic dimensions, and *Measure for Measure* is profoundly serious in its examination of moral problems. Equally, none of his tragedies is without humour: Hamlet is as witty as any of his comic heroes, *Macbeth* has its Porter, and *King Lear* its Fool. His greatest comic character, Falstaff, inhabits the history plays and *Henry V* ends with a marriage, while *Henry VI, Part III*, *Richard II* and *Richard III* culminate in the tragic deaths of their protagonists.

Although in performance Shakespeare's characters can give the impression of a superabundant reality, he is not a naturalistic dramatist. None of his plays is explicitly set in his own time. The action of few of them (except for the English histories) is set even partly in England (exceptions are *The Merry Wives of Windsor* and the Induction to *The Taming of the Shrew*). Italy is his favoured location. Most of his principal story-lines derive from printed writings; but the structuring and translation of these narratives into dramatic terms is Shakespeare's own, and he invents much additional material. Most of the plays contain elements of myth and legend, and many derive from ancient or more recent history or from romantic tales of ancient times and faraway places. All reflect his reading, often in close detail. Holinshed's *Chronicles* (1577, revised 1587), a great compendium of English, Scottish and Irish history, provided material for his English history plays. The *Lives of the Noble Grecians and Romans* by the Greek writer Plutarch, finely translated into English from the French by Sir Thomas North in 1579, provided much of the narrative material, and also a mass of verbal detail, for his plays about Roman history. Some plays are closely based on shorter individual works: *As You Like It*, for instance, on the novel *Rosalynde* (1590) by his near-contemporary Thomas Lodge (1558–1625), *The Winter's Tale* on *Pandosto* (1588) by his old rival Robert Greene (1558–92) and *Othello* on a story by the Italian Giraldi Cinthio (1504–73). And the language of his plays is permeated by the Bible, the Book of Common Prayer and the proverbial sayings of his day.

Shakespeare was popular with his contemporaries, but his commitment to the theatre and to the plays in performance is demonstrated by the fact that only about half of his plays appeared in print in his lifetime, in slim paperback volumes known as quartos, so called because they were made from printers' sheets folded twice to form four leaves (eight pages). None of them shows any sign that he was involved in their publication. For him, performance was the primary means of publication. The most frequently reprinted of his works were the nondramatic poems – the erotic *Venus and Adonis* and the more moralistic *The Rape of Lucrece*. The *Sonnets*, which appeared in 1609, under his name but possibly without his consent, were less successful, perhaps because the vogue for sonnet sequences, which peaked in the 1590s, had passed by then. They were not reprinted until 1640, and then only in garbled form along with poems by other writers. Happily, in 1623, seven years after he died, his colleagues John Heminges (1556–1630) and Henry Condell (d. 1627) published his collected plays, including eighteen that had not previously appeared in print, in the first Folio, whose name derives from the fact that the printers' sheets were folded only once to produce two leaves (four pages). Some of the quarto editions are badly printed, and the fact that some plays exist in two, or even three, early versions creates problems for editors. These are discussed in the Account of the Text in each volume of this series.

Shakespeare's plays continued in the repertoire until the Puritans closed the theatres in 1642. When performances resumed after the Restoration of the monarchy in 1660 many of the plays were not to the taste of the times, especially because their mingling of genres and failure to meet the requirements of poetic justice offended against the dictates of neoclassicism. Some, such as *The Tempest* (changed by John Dryden and William Davenant in 1667 to suit contemporary taste), *King Lear* (to which Nahum Tate gave a happy ending in 1681) and *Richard III* (heavily adapted by Colley Cibber in 1700 as a vehicle for his own talents), were extensively rewritten; others fell into neglect. Slowly they regained their place in the repertoire, and they continued to be reprinted, but it was not until the great actor David Garrick (1717–79) organized a spectacular jubilee in Stratford in 1769 that Shakespeare began to be regarded as a transcendental genius. Garrick's idolatry prefigured the enthusiasm of critics such as Samuel Taylor Coleridge (1772–1834) and William Hazlitt (1778–1830). Gradually Shakespeare's reputation spread abroad, to Germany, America, France and to other European countries.

During the nineteenth century, though the plays were generally still performed in heavily adapted or abbreviated versions, a large body of scholarship and criticism began to amass. Partly as a result of a general swing in education away from the teaching of Greek and Roman texts and towards literature written in English, Shakespeare became the object of intensive study in schools and universities. In the theatre, important turning points were the work in England of two theatre directors, William Poel (1852–1934) and his disciple Harley Granville-Barker (1877–1946), who showed that the application of knowledge, some of it newly acquired, of early staging conditions to performance of the plays could render the original texts viable in terms of the modern theatre. During the twentieth century appreciation of Shakespeare's work, encouraged by the availability of audio, film and video versions of the plays, spread around the world to such an extent that he can now be claimed as a global author.

The influence of Shakespeare's works permeates the English language. Phrases from his plays and poems – 'a tower of strength', 'green-eyed jealousy', 'a foregone conclusion' – are on the lips of people who may never have read him. They have inspired composers of songs, orchestral music and operas; painters and sculptors; poets, novelists and film-makers. Allusions to him appear in pop songs, in advertisements and in television shows. Some of his characters – Romeo and Juliet, Falstaff, Shylock and Hamlet – have acquired mythic status. He is valued for his humanity, his psychological insight, his wit and humour, his lyricism, his mastery of language, his ability to excite, surprise, move and, in the widest sense of the word, entertain audiences. He is the greatest of poets, but he is essentially a dramatic poet. Though his plays have much to offer to readers, they exist fully only in performance. In these volumes we offer individual introductions, notes on language and on specific points of the text, suggestions for further reading and information about how each work has been edited. In addition we include accounts of the ways in which successive generations of interpreters and audiences have responded to challenges and rewards offered by the plays. The Penguin Shakespeare series aspires to remove obstacles to understanding and to make pleasurable the reading of the work of the man who has done more than most to make us understand what it is to be human.

Stanley Wells

The Chronology of
Shakespeare's Works

A few of Shakespeare's writings can be fairly precisely dated. An allusion to the Earl of Essex in the chorus to Act V of *Henry V*, for instance, could only have been written in 1599. But for many of the plays we have only vague information, such as the date of publication, which may have occurred long after composition, the date of a performance, which may not have been the first, or a list in Francis Meres's book *Palladis Tamia*, published in 1598, which tells us only that the plays listed there must have been written by that year. The chronology of the early plays is particularly difficult to establish. Not everyone would agree that the first part of *Henry VI* was written after the third, for instance, or *Romeo and Juliet* before *A Midsummer Night's Dream*. The following table is based on the 'Canon and Chronology' section in *William Shakespeare: A Textual Companion*, by Stanley Wells and Gary Taylor, with John Jowett and William Montgomery (1987), where more detailed information and discussion may be found.

The Two Gentlemen of Verona	1590–91
The Taming of the Shrew	1590–91
Henry VI, Part II	1591
Henry VI, Part III	1591

Introduction

Much Ado About Nothing is a play as full of darkness as of sunlight, as much about repressed desire as about openly declared love, as interested in what cannot be spoken as in the delights of speaking. Shakespeare probably wrote it in 1598, and the only edition published before the first Folio of 1623 was printed in 1600. From 1600 his comic structures darkened further with *Twelfth Night* (1600–1601), *Measure for Measure* (1603) and *All's Well That Ends Well* (1604–5). Though we know little about its early performances, *Much Ado* seems to have been popular with audiences from the start. The first Quarto, printed only a year or two after the play was first performed, tells us that it had already been 'sundry times publicly acted by the right honourable, the Lord Chamberlain his servants'. While publishers naturally want to sell plays, they would have been unlikely to have made such a statement to an audience so close in time to the play's first performance if it had been a complete flop, so that this does give us some indication of the play's popularity in the year or two following its opening. Further evidence of its ongoing popularity is furnished by echoes of the play in Thomas Heywood's *Fair Maid of the Exchange* in 1607; and Leonard Digges's complimentary poem, printed in an edition of Shakespeare's poems in 1640,

takes this popularity down almost to the closing of the
theatres in 1642: 'let but Beatrice | And Benedick be
seen, lo in a trice | The Cockpit, galleries, boxes, all
are full'.

Its mixture of darkness and light, its traces of both
comic and tragic elements, though specific in some degree
to its own precise formulation of plot, character and
dialogue, are also characteristic of the dramatic composition of the period, as Samuel Johnson recognized in his
Preface to Shakespeare in 1765, in remarking upon the
difficulty of applying generic terms to Shakespeare's
'mingled drama'. For to categorize by genre is to recognize plays as conforming to certain rules, and, as Johnson
notes, those rules were not yet widely recognized or
followed in the sixteenth and early seventeenth centuries.
Shakespeare, Johnson argued, 'united the powers of
exciting laughter and sorrow . . . in one composition';
and neither he nor 'the players who in their edition [the
first Folio] divided our author's works into comedies,
histories, and tragedies, seem . . . to have distinguished
the three kinds by any very exact or definite ideas'.

Much Ado About Nothing seems to announce its know-
ingness about the mingling of laughter and sorrow from
the first, with its very consciously inserted, proverbial-
sounding statement by Leonato in the first scene: 'How
much better is it to weep at joy than to joy at weeping!'
(I.1.26–7). The play was written close in time to the 'green
world' comedies (those that involve a temporary retreat
into an idealized or unreal place), *As You Like It* and
Twelfth Night, yet critics have frequently chosen to discuss
it alongside the later, so-called 'problem plays', which,
with their hard-edged, often cynical tone and their resistance to full closure, claim the distinction of falling most
foul of generic categorization. *Much Ado*, partly by

seeming initially to court a more light-hearted response, opens up glimpses of horrors we even less expect to see – glimpses being the operative word, since so much is indirect, repressed or obliquely expressed in this play, and its signs so easily misread. As the title pun implies, the play's ado is about noting as well as nothing (pronounced similarly in Shakespeare's day), and false noting or failure to note can make something out of nothing or nothing out of something. The wordplay of the title also plays on the notion that all things are underpinned by the sexual relations between men and women and the need to learn to read, or note, the signs of desire correctly. As a man's sexual organ is, in Elizabethan slang, a 'thing' (Viola, faced with a duel in her male disguise in *Twelfth Night*, tells the audience aside that 'A little thing would make me tell them how much I lack of a man', III.4.293–4), so a woman's is 'no thing'; and 'nothing' can also be a term for a woman's virginity. 'Much ado' in the play is in one sense about 'nothing' in so far as all suspicions prove to be untrue; but it is also about the predictable and inevitable something, colloquially known as 'nothing', which is at the centre of both desire and suspicion.

The opening scene conveys a sense of edge from the start: an edge which is simultaneously the edge between generic categories and the edge between expression and repression. The scene begins with a letter and a messenger, both forms of expression conspicuously less direct than straightforward dialogue in a play. The messenger recounts both the military feats of Claudio and the tears of his uncle (a figure never heard of again in the play) on hearing of them, an account that provokes Leonato's portentous remark about weeping and joy. Beatrice's first utterance speaks of Benedick, but she refers to him by a name that seeks to mask her interest in him with a veneer of disdain: 'I pray you, is Signor Mountanto returned from the wars, or no?' (I.1.28–9). Her summary of what she remembers of his presence in Messina, however, is that he 'set up his bills here in Messina, and challenged Cupid at the flight' (36–7), that is, put up notices challenging Cupid to an archery contest. The remark is ambiguous. It could mean that Benedick set himself up as a great lover of women; it could mean the opposite, that he challenged Cupid to interest him in any woman; or it could mean that, in setting himself up as the lover of many women, he challenged Cupid to make him fall in love with any of them. Leonato's later joking about his sexual prowess (see p. xxv) suggests the last of these interpretations as the most likely, as do both Benedick's own insistence to Beatrice that 'it is certain I am loved of all ladies, only you excepted; and I would I could find in my heart that I had not a hard heart, for, truly, I love none' (I.1.116–19) and Don Pedro's later comment that Benedick 'hath twice or thrice cut Cupid's bow-string and the little hangman dare not shoot at him' (III.2.9–11). Whatever her meaning, the nature of Beatrice's preoccupation with him is signalled.

Her joking at Benedick's expense prompts Leonato's care to ensure that the messenger does not misread her: 'You must not, sir, mistake my niece. There is a kind of merry war betwixt Signor Benedick and her' (I.1.56–7). The warning is full of irony, since the plot is to hinge entirely around such mistaking of words and other signs. Indeed its ongoing concern with eavesdropping and misreporting mark it out from its sources, which hinge on a single act of deception, prominently shown. (The main sources are Ariosto's great narrative poem, *Orlando Furioso*, printed in 1516 and translated into English by

xxv   *Introduction*

John Harington in 1591, and a novella by Matteo Bandello, printed in 1554. Book II of Spenser's *Faerie Queene* may also have been an influence; while George Whetstone's *The Rocke of Regard* (1576), which Shakespeare may not have known, is notable for providing the only analogue to include a masque scene, see p. xxix below.) Most of the play's indirectness and concern over the ambiguity and possible misreading of signs carries a sexual charge, which becomes more conspicuous with the entrance of the men returning from war. First there is Leonato's strangely heavy-handed joke in response to Don Pedro's social enquiry:

DON PEDRO . . . I think this is your daughter.
LEONATO Her mother hath many times told me so (I.1.96–8);

and this in turn manufactures an opportunity for further allusion to Benedick's sexual conquests:

BENEDICK Were you in doubt, sir, that you asked her?
LEONATO Signor Benedick, no; for then were you a child.
   (99–100)

It is as though the play seeks to underline the point that all transactions, even the most apparently innocently social, are in fact grounded in sexual relations, as indeed its title implies. This becomes more explicit as an emergent new desire is more openly admitted to: Claudio's for Hero. Claudio's first question seeks reassurance about Hero's chastity ('Is she not a modest young lady?', 155), while Benedick's response takes the exchange into the more cynical realism of sexual economics and pragmatics:

BENEDICK Would you buy her, that you inquire after her?
CLAUDIO Can the world buy such a jewel?
BENEDICK Yea, and a case to put it into. (I.1.168–70)

Sexual jokes are a hallmark of the play, and women as well as men make them. Indeed eighteenth- and nineteenth-century critics found Beatrice's 'gratuitous impertinence and unseemly forwardness' (Henrietta Palmer, 1859) especially problematic. Amongst the men, however, the commonest motif of these sexual jokes is cuckoldry, the sexual betrayal of men by women, as Benedick's conversation with Claudio goes on to demonstrate:

That a woman conceived me, I thank her; that she brought me up, I likewise give her most humble thanks; but that I will have a recheat winded in my forehead, or hang my bugle in an invisible baldrick, all women shall pardon me. Because I will not do them the wrong to mistrust any, I will do myself the right to trust none; and the fine is, for the which I may go the finer, I will live a bachelor. (220–27)

The imagery is of hunting: Benedick refuses either to have a call to hounds sounded from his forehead (be known to all as a cuckold) or to hang his hunting horn in an invisible belt (a meaning less clear: either to be a secret cuckold, as most editors think, or perhaps to keep a lover himself). Either way, the imagery displays a cynical dismissal of marriage as a necessarily treacherous partnership. Thus, even as one young man seeks to speak seriously and admit to love with a view to marriage, another contests the idealistic potential of this moment by introducing a perspective that automatically links sexual desire with distrust of women. By the time Claudio

makes his prolonged and lyrical claim to 'soft and delicate desires' (282) in verse at the end of the scene, a more
lewd, suspicious and cynical point of view is already
impossible to dismiss.

Claudio's confession of desire constitutes almost the
first lines of verse in a play remarkable for its predomi-
nance of prose. As one nineteenth-century commentator,
'D. G.', writes, 'This comedy has far fewer passages of
poetical beauty than almost any other production of
Shakespeare'; yet its prose is not an index of plainness,
but rather of rhetorical flourish and patterning.
Benedick's cuckoldry joke above, for example, is the
second of two consecutive sets of utterances which are
patterned thus: Claudio/Don Pedro speaks; Don
Pedro/Claudio answers, with a response of equal length
and similar grammatical construction; and Benedick caps
both with a lengthier verbal display:

CLAUDIO That I love her, I feel.

DON PEDRO That she is worthy, I know.

BENEDICK That I neither feel how she should be loved, nor
    know how she should be worthy, is the opinion that fire
    cannot melt out of me; I will die in it at the stake.

DON PEDRO Thou wast ever an obstinate heretic in the despite
    of beauty.

CLAUDIO And never could maintain his part but in the force
    of his will.

BENEDICK That a woman conceived me . . . (211–20; see above)

The patterning is conspicuous and comes across as highly
self-conscious. The conducting of social relations as a
series of theatrical verbal set pieces suggests a brittleness
and shallowness about the interaction. Such rhetoric,
though enjoyable for both participants and audience,

highlights conversation as manufactured more for the purpose of display than communication. And the prevalence of jokes in particular, although great fun for the audience, also shows how far the society depicted in this play seeks to play on the surface of things while avoiding clear and direct confrontation.

Claudio's lyrical utterance, then, constitutes almost the first lines in verse, but not quite; for the dialogue first turns to verse at the point where Claudio and Don Pedro are left alone and Claudio speaks of requiring Don Pedro's help to 'do me good' (I.1.269), then goes on to establish by careful enquiry that Hero is Leonato's only heir. An audience now, unaccustomed to attending explicitly to the alternation of verse and prose, may or may not register the move into verse; but an earlier audience, for whom a predominantly verse-drama was the norm, and who understood and listened for the distinct pleasures of verse and prose, would certainly notice the shift, especially as it is scripted to follow on from the exit of the witty Benedick. There is irony about the move into verse at this point, however. An audience might expect Claudio to turn to Don Pedro at this moment with an idealistic declaration of love. Instead the move is into a different kind of earnestness: a hard-headed financial enquiry. The realist viewpoint thus undercuts and circumscribes what might have been a romantic moment of youthful sincerity; and it does so even as the play moves into verse, thus highlighting to the ear everything that the utterance might be expected to do but deliberately does not do. What the verse conveys, far from a private confession of love, is that, even in private, the considerations of the realist precede the admission of love. Claudio, having checked with Benedick that he believes Hero to be as chaste as she looks, now checks with Don

Pedro that her apparent status as sole heir is also to be believed. So it is not merely Benedick's jokes, but also Claudio's own sequence of thought, that take the first confession of love out of idealist territory. No one trusts appearances or women in this play, it seems, and when there is a choice to be made between the two, distrust of women is the stronger. Don John's plot to discredit Hero proceeds from the fact that, when appearances seem to signal that women are *not* to be trusted, all men except the Friar, from lover to father to friends and observers, instantly trust the truth of the visible surface.

In terms of plot as well as prose, the play is a brittle and brilliant accumulation of surfaces. Its mode of being is emblematized, or given symbolic form, in the masque of Act II, scene 1. A masque (or as earlier spelling more commonly has it, 'mask') was a form of courtly dancing and/or show, usually initiated through the sudden irruption of a group of elaborately costumed and disguised dancers into the company and their taking of dancing partners from the assembled group. The famous Tudor chronicler Edward Hall, describing its introduction to the English court in 1512, sees it as a somewhat risky pastime, brought from Italy, and notes that on that occasion 'some that knew the fashion of it refused'. This sense of risk carries over in Shakespeare's use of masques in his early plays, where he usually portrays them as creating a licensed space for a slightly more edgy engagement between the sexes than would be acceptable in everyday life. Like the eavesdropping, the masquing is Shakespeare's addition to his sources (Whetstone's *The Rocke of Regard*, as noted above, includes a masque scene, but was probably not known to Shakespeare), a sure sign that it has a conscious and deliberate function. As Harold Jenkins has shown (in an essay in Fabian and

Tetzeli von Rosador (eds.), *Shakespeare: Text, Language, Criticism*), the masked dance 'adumbrates a pattern which reflects the larger action of a marriage made, broken, and remade'; and Beatrice herself has a set piece beforehand telling Hero (and, more importantly, the audience) that the action that takes men and women through courtship and into marriage is patterned like a series of dances:

> wooing, wedding, and repenting, is as a Scotch jig, a measure, and a cinquepace: the first suit is hot and hasty, like a Scotch jig, and full as fantastical; the wedding, mannerly-modest, as a measure, full of state and ancientry; and then comes repentance and, with his bad legs, falls into the cinquepace faster and faster, till he sink into his grave. (II.1.64–71)

Claudio is not the only one to express a realism in relation to marriage that is in tension with romantic ideas about love.

It is not merely that the symmetry and movement of dance mimic the larger patterns of courtship and marriage, however, but that masquing mimics the particular motions of desire as they are enacted in *this* play. The point may be made by comparing this masque with the masque in *Romeo and Juliet*, which functions to bring sudden desire to a moment of confession and completeness, formally enacted through the lyric intensity and totality of sonnet form and visually enacted and confirmed through two kisses (*Romeo and Juliet*, I.5.93–110). Desire in *Much Ado*, by contrast, is never given such open space, such frankness or such completion. It focuses instead on a series of fragmentary moments as the dance rotates the couples round the stage in sequence; on the humour inherent in seeing through disguise and the opportunities that offers for veiled insults; and on risqué remarks that play on

the edge of revealing desire while never quite openly
confessing to it. When Beatrice and Benedick come
together, the event is scripted to tease the audience, as
they themselves tease each other, with the question of
whether they recognize each other. Normal practice would
have only the incoming revellers masked (in this case,
then, Benedick, but not Beatrice), though stage directions
in the Quarto and Folio do not really clarify this point
one way or the other (see further An Account of the Text
and Harold Jenkins's essay). The dialogue that follows
shows Beatrice speaking only of Benedick, either teasing
him knowingly, or revealing, less knowingly, her constant
preoccupation with him:

BEATRICE That I was disdainful, and that I had my good wit
    out of the 'Hundred Merry Tales' – well, this was Signor
    Benedick that said so.
BENEDICK What's he?
BEATRICE I am sure you know him well enough.
BENEDICK Not I, believe me.
BEATRICE Did he never make you laugh?
BENEDICK I pray you, what is he?
BEATRICE Why, he is the Prince's jester, a very dull fool; only
    his gift is in devising impossible slanders. None but libertines
    delight in him, and the commendation is not in his wit, but
    in his villainy; for he both pleases men and angers them,
    and then they laugh at him and beat him. I am sure he is
    in the fleet; I would he had boarded me. (II.1.115–29)

Either way, the experience centres on sexual tension
between the two. When Beatrice utters the wish 'I would
he had boarded me', it is as though the utterance is almost
forced out by a desire that takes control of her against
her will. It seems to slip out of the carefully controlled

exchange of formally touching bodies and witty repartee
to make a space for the freer, more open kind of interaction those forms of exchange repress. No editor's note
in any modern edition offers any plausible way of reading
this remark as making innocent sense in the context. Its
primary meaning, whether one takes 'board' to be a
metaphor (as in boarding a ship) or more literally, as it
is used by Sir Toby in *Twelfth Night* to gloss the word
'accost' ('front her, board her, woo her, assail her',
I.3.53–4), points to Beatrice's wish to be either wooed or
bedded by Benedick. But Beatrice and Benedick do not
seize the masque passionately and voluntarily, as do
Romeo and Juliet, to pour out their hearts. They draw
near, pull back, negotiate for space, skirt round the centre
of their desire – and desire seems to break through the
social frame despite them.

The masque is further emblematic of the play's wider
concerns in that it becomes the focus of much noting
(how does this man move? what does he say? who is he?
who does he speak for?), as well as of much ado about
nothing (the brief mistaking and deception that allow,
first, Hero and Leonato to believe that Don Pedro will
woo Hero, and, second, Claudio to believe that Don Pedro
has wooed and won Hero for himself, are soon corrected).
In line with the concerns of the title, as sexual relations
are about both desire and possession, so there must be
much noting of both the signs of desire and the signs that
possession may or may not be secure. The noting arises
out of both desire and suspicion and focuses on nothing:
that is, simultaneously, women's virginity, their sexual
organs, their desire, their potential wantonness and
nothing at all. That 'nothing', then (in the sense that all
suspicions prove untrue), is also the very something which
is at the heart of both legitimate and faithful marriage

and illegitimate, wanton relations. Hence the play's seemingly endless sequence of jokes about cuckoldry.

Hence, too, the plot that makes a bastard seek opportunities to inhibit the fulfilment of true and loving marriage. Here again Shakespeare breaks with his sources in substituting the otherwise motiveless Don John for a rival lover in the source plots. The point changes from a personal motivation, jealousy, to a more generalized and social cause: bastardy opposes the movement towards marriage with almost mindless, automatic force. The substitution creates a tightly coherent focus on sexuality, desire, the attempt to constrain it and the places where it escapes those constraints, the 'nothing', in short, which the play's title puts at its centre. For the bastard is legally the son of nobody: morally an outrage, and socially an outsider. He is the child of fornication or adultery, the monstrous product of unconstrained sexual desire and often, besides, a by-product of cuckoldry. He makes double and bitter sense of the play's obsession with horns and horniness and he emblematizes its focus on nothing. Don John's bastardy is not incidental (his name may indeed have been chosen in order to call to mind the famous illegitimate son of the Emperor Charles V and brother of Philip II of Spain, Don John of Austria), nor does his action need any greater motive than that of his despised position and the narrative logic by which bastardy opposes itself to legitimacy. When Edmund in *King Lear* expresses the view that unnatural behaviour is only to be expected of one unnaturally begotten, he is giving utterance not to an individual opinion but to a view that was current in legal texts of the time. *Much Ado*'s bastard, regularly named as 'Bastard' rather than 'Don John' in many of the Quarto speech-prefixes, is congenitally false: not merely the offspring of a polluted coupling, but, in Michael Neill's phrase, 'an epitome of the counterfeit' (*Putting History to the Question: Power, Politics, and Society in English Renaissance Drama* (2000)). He thus brings together the violent undersides of noting and nothing, deceit and unpoliced desire, representing the degree to which the underside is natural and necessary, as opposed to accidental.

Don John's devising of false shows to display apparent betrayal is thus also a variation on masque form. Each is a theatrical set piece, staging a set of relations which have no depth or duration. One is playful, even risky, while its underside is deliberately and disruptively negative. Couples join hands formally and symmetrically in the masque, enacting a brief moment of union in the same way as the scene staged at the window by Don John fleetingly enacts a seeming union between Hero and Borachio. Yet this show of Don John's differs from the numerous other shows in the play by being reported rather than performed; and here again Shakespeare can be seen making a significant alteration to his sources, all of which give this false show more substance. Directors who insert such a scene miss the point here. Shakespeare's aim is precisely to emphasize the insubstantiality of this show by contrast with all the other shows within a self-consciously metatheatrical, or theatrically self-concious, play. These, however insubstantial they may seem, turn out to be very substantial indeed.

The play proceeds through a marked sequence of overtly theatrical scenes, stage-managed by characters within the plot, the most seemingly insubstantial being the parallel garden scenes in which Benedick and Beatrice are persuaded by contrived eavesdropping that each loves the other. Benedick and Beatrice are themselves additions to Shakespeare's sources, and these two theatrical scenes are thus also additional to the sources. They may seem insubstantial in as far as they seem to reduce love to something contrived with a simple, paper-thin device; but, as the play makes us understand, it is only because the substance of love is already present, unadmitted between these two sparring partners, that persuading them to recognize it is so easy. The evidence on both sides is there before the garden scenes, first in Act I, scene 1, where Benedick's response to Claudio's opinion that Hero is 'the sweetest lady that ever I looked on' states a plain preference for Beatrice: 'I can see yet without spectacles, and I see no such matter; there's her cousin, an she were not possessed with a fury, exceeds her as much in beauty as the first of May doth the last of December' (175–80); and later in Act II, scene 1, when Beatrice, taxed by Don Pedro for upsetting Benedick with her jests ('you have lost the heart of Signor Benedick'), responds in sombre vein with remembrance of a shared past: 'Indeed, my lord, he lent it me awhile, and I gave him use for it, a double heart for his single one. Marry, once before he won it of me with false dice, therefore your grace may well say I have lost it' (253–8).

The fact that the gulling scenes (those that seek to trick Beatrice and Benedick) take place in a garden also sends out its own signals, especially in a play where precise location is otherwise unimportant. (An earlier generation of editors would identify a setting for each scene, but unless the text calls attention to location as important, it may be taken as relatively fluid.) In these scenes, Shakespeare is careful to identify location. Benedick, who is first to be gulled, opens Act II, scene 3, by sending a boy to his chamber to bring a book 'hither to me in the orchard' (4), and, when he sees Don Pedro and Claudio approaching, he announces his intention to hide 'in the

arbour' (II.3.34). The next scene, which follows on with
the gulling of Beatrice, opens with Hero bidding Margaret
'whisper' to Beatrice that Hero and Ursula

> Walk in the orchard, and our whole discourse
> Is all of her; say that thou overheardst us,
> And bid her steal into the pleachèd bower,
> Where honeysuckles, ripened by the sun,
> Forbid the sun to enter. (III.1.5–9)

The term 'pleachèd bower' not only seems to specify the
same location as Benedick's 'arbour', so that the audience can see these symmetrical deceits played out in
symmetrical staging, but echoes Antonio's earlier
mistaking of Don Pedro's intention, when he tells
Leonato that he heard Don Pedro and Claudio talking
of the former's love for Hero as they walked 'in a thick-
pleached alley in mine orchard' (I.2.8–9). Shakespeare
uses the word 'pleached', meaning intertwined or covered
over with interlaced boughs, only once outside *Much
Ado*, so his use of it twice in this play is striking. It
emphasizes envelopment, concealment and privacy.
Gardens already had a long literary tradition, going back
to the biblical Song of Solomon, of serving as the location for erotic meetings and fantasies and as metaphors
for the female 'nothing' which is so central to this play.
Repetition of these areas of garden as 'pleached' encour-
ages our awareness of their potential erotic associations,
while at the same time highlighting the covered and
concealed nature of that eroticism.

Intervening between these shows and the highly
theatrical scene of Hero's denunciation in the church are
two scenes underlining action as performance by virtue
of seeming to show areas 'behind the scene'. First Don

John invites his audience to the show he has planned: 'Go but with me tonight, you shall see her chamber-window entered, even the night before her wedding-day' (III.2.101–3). Following that, the Watch are then introduced into the play for the first time, and Dogberry tells them how to play their parts, first giving the constable of the watch his identifying prop, a lantern, and then giving instructions on how a watchman should behave. The comedy of the scene lies in the foolishness of both the questions and the answers concerning how to play the part, including the sage endorsement of conspicuous misunderstanding of the role, as, for example, in this exchange:

FIRST WATCHMAN We will rather sleep than talk; we know what belongs to a watch.
DOGBERRY Why, you speak like an ancient and most quiet watchman, for I cannot see how sleeping should offend . . . (III.3.37–40)

The psychoanalyst Sigmund Freud argued that Dogberry constituted a convenient figure for repression of the unconscious. Indeed, the play's clowning scenes incorporate its central concern with repression as a structural feature, cutting away from impending climaxes such as the window scene, and substituting extended delay and comic mistaking for them. The window scene is anticipated and described on either side of this interlude, but never appears. What appears in its place is a group of bumbling policemen seeking to leave drunks well alone, let thieves steal out of their company and offend no man. The logic of the scenic construction is both comic and ironic: while the social elite of Messina is engrossed in an apparent failure to police its own young women, a plot constructed by the very one of its own whom it actually fails to police, its bastard, is discovered by the accidental bumbling of that society's very police force. Since Hero's apparent transgression, furthermore, is in fact merely a matter of appearance, created through the devising of a fake show, the uncovering of that fakery through a further, and much more improbable, mistaking adds another dimension to the symmetries of plot.

Verbally, too, the comic scenes provide a prismatic reflection of the main plot. Dogberry's love of the sound of his own voice plays another variation on the ongoing surface banter of the male protagonists and the verbal fireworks of Beatrice and Benedick, while his characteristic verbal signature of mixing up words with others that sound like them (now called 'malapropism', after a later character in Sheridan's play *The Rivals*, who did the same thing), picks up the play's central emphasis on misprision, or mistaking. Borachio's drunken ramblings immediately following in this same scene take the parodic engagement with the main plot even further, relating again to both verbal and narrative elements in the plot. The way his metaphor of the 'deformed thief', fashion, is transformed by the watchmen into a known criminal ('I know that Deformed; 'a has been a vile thief this seven year; 'a goes up and down like a gentleman. I remember his name', III.3.122–4) constitutes not only a small comic masterpiece, but also a reflection on the central concerns of the play. As the dialogue develops, beating the words 'deformed' and 'fashion' to death, the audience may realize that an important point is being hammered home:

BORACHIO Seest thou not, I say, what a deformed thief this
     fashion is, how giddily 'a turns about all the hot bloods
     between fourteen and five-and-thirty, sometimes fash-

ioning them like Pharaoh's soldiers in the reechy painting,
sometime like god Bel's priests in the old church-window,
sometime like the shaven Hercules in the smirched worm-
eaten tapestry, where his codpiece seems as massy as his
club?

CONRADE All this I see; and I see that the fashion wears out
more apparel than the man. But art not thou thyself giddy
with the fashion too, that thou hast shifted out of thy tale
into telling me of the fashion? (127–38)

Despite the seemingly random nature of this exchange,
its mode of verbal engagement resembles the witty
repartee of the play's social elite. The bastard who is at
the centre of the deceit indeed represents a deformity in
social practice; and the insistence here on fashion, together
with the suggestive link between fashion and conspicuous, obtrusive desire (in the shape of Hercules, the
bastard), come to seem emblematic of a play in which
making a good show, whether in dress, in verbal style or
in the masking of desire and the cloaking of its escapes,
is a central activity, whereas going against the fashion,
when it becomes visible, whether in matters of style or
more deeply embedded social practices, must be policed.

Borachio's reported account of the omitted window
scene shows exactly how Hero and Claudio have been
set up by Don John and anticipates the church scene with
hard clarity: 'away went Claudio enraged; swore he would
meet her, as he was appointed, next morning at the temple,
and there, before the whole congregation, shame her with
what he saw o'er night, and send her home again without
a husband' (III.3.153–7). As the scene ends with the
watchmen still muttering about finding 'Deformed', the
next scene cuts with pointed dramatic irony to one in
which the women prepare for the church scene, one that

we now know will not be what the women anticipate. As talk of Hero's wedding dress prompts Hero to admit that her 'heart is exceedingly heavy', Margaret's openly sexual joke ''Twill be heavier soon, by the weight of a man' (III.4.22–4) drops hollowly, echoing the sexual banter that we have so often seen in the male society of the play, and now sounds with such pathos in this women's scene, where female vulnerability is so much sharper in the audience's imagination than in the characters' awareness. The scene closes with emphasis on the ongoing back-stage preparations for the anticipated spectacle:

URSULA Madam, withdraw; the Prince, the Count, Signor
    Benedick, Don John, and all the gallants of the town, are
    come to fetch you to church.
HERO Help to dress me, good coz, good Meg, good Ursula.
    (86–90)

Yet again the scene cuts back to the Watch, here announcing their arrest to Leonato. It is inserted here partly to extend the suspense between these backstage preparations and the 'big scene', allowing the audience longer to savour the tension between Don John's deceit, its closeness to discovery and the enactment of the wedding. It also reminds us, with its wordiness, how tedious, as Leonato here says himself, words can be. Again we are reminded of both the importance and the limitations of verbal exchange: how difficult it can be to read; how easily it can be misread; how much of a show it can make; how far the show can be substituting for something else kept back, whether repressed, deliberately masked or merely postponed.

The entry for the church scene must include some degree of spectacle, since Hero is now wearing the very

dress so much praised in Act III, scene 4 as better even
than the Duchess of Milan's. Yet there is also a current
that works against the slow and formal ceremonial that
we expect, evident from Leonato's opening lines: 'Come,
Friar Francis, be brief; only to the plain form of marriage,
and you shall recount their particular duties afterwards'
(IV.i.1–3). The Friar's next line, accordingly, is the prompt
for the core words of the marriage ceremony: 'I do'; but
the ceremony at once breaks down with shocking speed
and a change of register from comedy to melodrama:

FRIAR FRANCIS You come hither, my lord, to marry this lady.
CLAUDIO No.

The scene moves from the near-comic discomfort of
Leonato's joking, through the brutality of Claudio's
rejection, to the melodrama of Leonato's call for a dagger
and Hero's swoon. The terminology used of Hero
becomes increasingly disturbing and out of place in a
comedy: she is a 'rotten orange', 'an approvèd wanton',
'a common stale', 'more intemperate . . . [than] animals |
That rage in savage sensuality'. Her own father wishes
her dead, outdoing even Claudio and Don Pedro in his
disgust with her 'foul tainted flesh' (30, 42, 63, 57–9, 141).
    It is partly because Messina is a place of such glit-
tering surfaces, a place where social masks are usually so
carefully maintained, that the tenor of this language is
so shocking. In the wake of the patterned, posturing prose
that has scripted most of the social encounters of the play
thus far, 'Give not this rotten orange to your friend' marks
a change of rhetoric and a change in the nature of interaction. In a previous remark, an orange figures within a
classically witty pun on Beatrice's part, though in a
context that proves to be prophetic in its display of

distrust. Claudio is looking despondent on that occasion because he believes Don Pedro to have wooed Hero for himself instead of for Claudio, as promised; Beatrice, punning on civil and Seville, and pointing to the traditional yellow colour of jealousy, jokes that Claudio 'is neither sad, nor sick, nor merry, nor well; but civil count, civil as an orange, and something of that jealous complexion' (II.1.269–71). That overactive jealousy is recalled here in the bitter violence of this image, which leaves wit and wordplay behind. It is as clear and direct as it is possible to be, cutting through the verbal fencing that has filled up all spaces to this point. The line is scripted to create space following it: the pause should be audible.

This high tension and vicious feeling around Hero's supposed sexual promiscuity is the underside of the irruption of Beatrice's desire in the masque scene. There, what was briefly exposed, in its most winning and attractive form, was the way sexual desire is so strong that it slips out when the temporary licence of masque relaxes the usual constraints on social behaviour. Here, in the rejection of Hero, we see the full extent of what is really unleashed for this society and this class by the prospect of sexual desire escaping its social restrictions. The temporary licence of masque, which allows a brief glimpse of desires normally kept hidden, is one thing; but the possibility of real licence, of desire that has fully escaped the social frame, not just in a passing remark but in physical consummation outside marriage, infringes accepted boundaries in a way that cannot be tolerated. And, as the act of fornication is itself so far beyond the bounds of what is acceptable in this society, so the language of that same society breaks the bounds of all its own proprieties in having to confront such an act. Where marriage is the binding formal structure that legitimates desire and gives shape to society, an act which allows desire to transgress legitimacy completely cuts across and disables all expected modes of social interaction. Critics often focus on the outrageousness of Claudio's behaviour; but what must also be acknowledged is that Claudio's language and behaviour are endorsed by the other men of his social class, including even Hero's own father. And the whole of society stands in clear opposition to the figure designated as excluded from the social order: the bastard, who represents the taboo that can scarcely be spoken and yet is repeatedly indirectly expressed in the play's ongoing current of cuckoldry jokes and always visible in the bastard's own marginal status (a status that can be made very physically visible in performance through costume, delivery and the way the actor occupies stage-space). There is a logical and thematic neatness to the fact that a bastard seeks to bring shame and confusion on the group whose social legitimacy excludes him by seeking to expose an act of almost unimaginable illegitimacy at its centre and at the most intolerable point, just before an unwitting young lover ties himself irrevocably to the perpetrator of such foulness.

Into this sharp division between men and women, however, where men close ranks against women's apparent treachery and women close ranks in loyalty that knows better than appearances, comes the relationship between Beatrice and Benedick. In a play where, I have argued, desire is characteristically repressed and speech characteristically seeks to mask rather than to express true feeling, the encounter between Beatrice and Benedick in the church scene is marked out by its truthfulness, and hence its difference in dramatic register, from the rest of the play. Up to this point we have seen Beatrice and

Benedick seek out each other's company, taunt each other publicly, speak of each other privately and fall prey with equal speed to the notion that they are loved by each other. We have even seen Benedick once speak seriously to Beatrice, only to be mocked:

BEATRICE Against my will I am sent to bid you come in to dinner.
BENEDICK Fair Beatrice, I thank you for your pains.
BEATRICE I took no more pains for those thanks than you take pains to thank me; if it had been painful, I would not have come (II.3.239–44);

and we have seen Beatrice once speak seriously to herself of love:

And, Benedick, love on; I will requite thee,
Taming my wild heart to thy loving hand.
If thou dost love, my kindness shall incite thee
To bind our loves up in a holy band. (III.1.111–14)

We may also have registered the fact that, as each speaks seriously of love, prose turns to verse and seems almost to mock their former witty selves and to parody their new-found status as lovers.

Now the church scene brings new dimensions to verse and prose, to the seriousness of Beatrice and Benedick and to the register of the play. Having opened with the standard male banter in prose, as Leonato directs the Friar to be brief and dares to make Claudio's answer for him when the formal question about any impediments to the marriage is pronounced, the scene moves into verse at the point where Claudio begins to play out his formal rejection of Hero. It is Benedick's tender concern for

Beatrice and her response, the first lines exchanged without mockery or irony between them, that change the verse back into prose, which thereby gains a new earnestness and honesty:

BENEDICK Lady Beatrice, have you wept all this while?
BEATRICE Yea, and I will weep a while longer. (IV.1.253–4)

The open admission of tension and hurt on Beatrice's part takes the play into a new space where the masks are off and concealment gives way to expression. For characters so habituated to masking and surface play it is a dangerous place, and the exchange is fragile, tense and barbed:

BENEDICK Surely I do believe your fair cousin is wronged.
BEATRICE Ah, how much might the man deserve of me that
    would right her!
BENEDICK Is there any way to show such friendship?
BEATRICE A very even way, but no such friend.
BENEDICK May a man do it?
BEATRICE It is a man's office, but not yours. (257–63)

Given the play's care to show a society in which the men are war veterans and male swagger is central to self-definition, it is remarkable that Benedick is provoked by this last remark not to anger but to a declaration of love: 'I do love nothing in the world so well as you; is not that strange?' Beatrice is more guarded, but is gradually brought to admit her own love, an admission that prompts Benedick to tender self-parody in claiming the position of the romantic lover: 'Come, bid me do anything for thee'; and Beatrice to the most famously forthright line of the play: 'Kill Claudio' (264–5, 284–5). The reason this line can provoke laughter from an audience is that it is so unexpected. Benedick's half-humorous question has taken us not quite back into the defensive wit of the early repartee, but at least towards a reminder of the half-rueful, self-mocking resignation with which he accepted a lover's role: 'No, the world must be peopled. When I said I would die a bachelor, I did not think I should live till I were married' (II.3.234–6).

To move, then, from a mock-Romeo moment into the absolute seriousness of Beatrice's answer is to move not just from one kind of relationship into another, but, from the audience's point of view, from one kind of play into another (though 'Give not this rotten orange to your friend' anticipates the change – both lines are scripted to produce a shocked pause in place of endless, rapid verbal to-and-fro). After such a moment, things can never be the same again. If Benedick's confession of love signalled a new truthfulness, this signals an even deeper and more trusting risk-taking on Beatrice's part. In responding to Benedick's mock-romantic pose with a command that allows that romantic posture, even momentarily, to be taken seriously, she risks not only making her own feelings totally visible to Benedick, but exposing her complete reliance on him. Since she is not a man, she must, like any self-respecting romance heroine, rely on a man to perform the male version of what she sees as the necessary and appropriate action to redeem such slander: 'eat his heart in the market-place' (IV.1.302). Yet we know that Beatrice is not a romance heroine, and that the play is nevertheless a comedy: by its own admission, 'much ado about nothing'. So the moment is compromised by its surroundings, starkly clear-cut and earnest, cutting through the chattering, unstoppable wordiness that is clever, witty, social, masking/masquing Messina. Benedick takes up the challenge, thus answering and covering Beatrice's self-exposure. It is the moral equivalent of taking her in his arms, a moment still postponed, indeed explicitly shied away from in the farewell Benedick does take: 'I will challenge him. I will kiss your hand, and so I leave you' (326–7).

This plain and forceful speaking, however, is a brief interlude. The play's calculated wordiness, and the emphasis on words as surfaces, resumes immediately in the next scene with Dogberry's opening malapropism: 'Is our whole dissembly appeared?' (IV.2.1). Yet, as in the earlier exchange about the deformed thief, fashion, two words are prominent in this scene, 'villain' and 'ass'; and, through all the mistaking, two concepts, both blindingly obvious, emerge with absolute clarity: Don John is a villain and Dogberry is an ass. Yet there is a perverse pleasure in the combination of the blindingly obvious with extended misinterpretation of words. The plot has been concerned with the difficulty of reading signs and making them signify clearly; the verbal exchanges of the central protagonists have regularly played with the way in which wit, irony and wordplay present words as flashy objects on view rather than transparent carriers of meaning. Now, when clowns take so many words to clarify truths so self-evident, the audience can begin to feel that clarity and revelation are imminent.

Act V, however, opens with the elite counterpart of the comic play with words. Dogberry has spoken in slowly circling, self-important prose to call attention to himself and his position:

I am a wise fellow, and, which is more, an officer; and, which is more, a householder; and, which is more, as pretty a piece of flesh as any is in Messina; and one that knows

the law, go to; and a rich fellow enough, go to; and a fellow
that hath had losses; and one that hath two gowns and
everything handsome about him. (IV.2.77–83)

Now Leonato indulges in equally extended verse to
underline his position as grieving father:

Bring me a father that so loved his child,
Whose joy of her is overwhelmed like mine,
And bid him speak of patience;
Measure his woe the length and breadth of mine,
And let it answer every strain for strain,
And thus for thus, and such a grief for such,
In every lineament, branch, shape, and form;
If such a one will smile and stroke his beard,
And, sorry wag, cry 'hem!' when he should groan,
Patch grief with proverbs, make misfortune drunk
With candle-wasters – bring him yet to me,
And I of him will gather patience. (V.1.8–19)

Hearing this speech of grief, it can be quite hard for the
audience to remember that Hero is not in fact dead, and
that Leonato knows it. (Readers may wish to consider
Barbara Everett's suggested emendation of 'And, sorry
wag' to 'Bid sorrow's wag', in Cordner, Holland and
Kerrigan (eds.), *English Comedy*.) But giving full space
to the emblematic representation of grief is important to
the shape of the play, for the second half of Act V, scene
1 returns to the joking and male camaraderie dominant
in so many of the scenes prior to Claudio's outburst in
the church, and the comic resolution of the Hero–Claudio
plot must not be completely drained of seriousness.
Benedick's challenge comes perilously close to doing
precisely that, since Claudio and Don Pedro utterly refuse

to take him seriously. Not only does Claudio find the idea of a challenge richly comic, but Benedick's reply, spoken in utter seriousness, nevertheless contains clear verbal echoes of Dogberry's insistence that Don John be written down a villain and the exchange between Margaret and Hero about the heavy hearts and heavy bodies:

BENEDICK Shall I speak a word in your ear?
CLAUDIO God bless me from a challenge!
BENEDICK (*aside to Claudio*) You are a villain; I jest not. I will
    make it good how you dare, with what you dare, and when
    you dare. Do me right, or I will protest your cowardice.
    You have killed a sweet lady, and her death shall fall heavy
    on you. Let me hear from you. (V.i.140–46)

The scripting of such echoes is a risky stratagem, but one that brings together the play's characteristic combination of laughter and sorrow with sharp poignancy. The renewal of cuckold jokes treads the same edge, especially since the seemingly cuckolded Claudio is himself a participant:

DON PEDRO But when shall we set the savage bull's horns on
    the sensible Benedick's head?
CLAUDIO Yes, and text underneath, 'Here dwells Benedick the
    married man'? (174–7)

And this is turn scripts an even more explicit reminder of earlier joking at Benedick's expense in the first scene of the play, in an exchange which gives Claudio the cuckold joke to crack:

DON PEDRO Well, as time shall try:
    'In time the savage bull doth bear the yoke.'

BENEDICK The savage bull may; but if ever the sensible
Benedick bear it, pluck off the bull's horns and set them in
my forehead, and let me be vilely painted; and in such great
letters as they write 'Here is good horse to hire', let them
signify under my sign 'Here you may see Benedick the
married man.'

CLAUDIO If this should ever happen, thou wouldst be horn-
mad. (I.1.240–49)

Joking, especially about horns, has been the characteristic mode of a play intent on showing a society that
represses desire. On this occasion, Benedick, now familiar
with a more open and plain-speaking expression, strikes
a distance from the elite and military male grouping with
which he was previously aligned, dismissing their taste-
less humour and Claudio's youth:

Fare you well, boy; you know my mind. I will leave you
now to your gossip-like humour; you break jests as braggarts do their blades, which, God be thanked, hurt not. (*To
Don Pedro*) My lord, for your many courtesies I thank you;
I must discontinue your company. Your brother the Bastard
is fled from Messina. You have among you killed a sweet
and innocent lady. For my Lord Lackbeard there, he and I
shall meet; and till then, peace be with him. (V.1.178–86)

The structure crosses over in the next two scenes,
which present Beatrice and Benedick joking together
again, though with more honesty than before, and
Claudio, Don Pedro and Balthasar in a highly serious
and formal scene which brings the play's emphasis on
theatricality to the fore again. Lighted tapers, mourning
dress and a monumental setting underline the ritual aspect
of the scene, as does the fact that Claudio reads Hero's

epitaph from a script. Nothing could be further from the
improvised wit that has characterized so many meetings
of this group. Verbal form too stands out from the rest
of the play, since it is neither prose nor blank verse, but
rhyming verse, conspicuous by its difference on its rare
appearances. The song, moreover, answers the play's only
previous song, just before the deception of Benedick is
begun, and employs the same singer, Balthasar, on both
occasions:

> Sigh no more, ladies, sigh no more,
>   Men were deceivers ever,
> One foot in sea and one on shore,
>   To one thing constant never:
> Then sigh not so, but let them go,
>   And be you blithe and bonny,
> Converting all your sounds of woe
>   Into Hey nonny, nonny. (II.3.60–67)

In the earlier scene the song's prominence is highlighted
by some very extended wordplay on notes, noting and
nothing in the preceding conversation. The link between
noting, deception and sexuality could scarcely be more
heavily underlined. This song, by contrast, marks a turn
to constancy, a shift away from changeable fashion and
the noting of surfaces to a new willingness to take things
on faith. It seeks pardon, enacts repentance and gives
new weight to the 'heaviness' already played on since the
preparations for the wedding:

> Pardon, goddess of the night,
> Those that slew thy virgin knight;
> For the which, with songs of woe,
> Round about her tomb they go.

Midnight, assist our moan,
Help us to sigh and groan,
　　Heavily, heavily.
Graves yawn and yield your dead,
Till death be utterèd,
　　Heavily, heavily. (V.3.12–21)

As ritual performs repentance, theatricality begins to acquire a positive value. Claudio's willingness to perform an annual rite of mourning for the woman who has seemingly died as a consequence of his slander initiates a practice of penitence which seems the more powerful and serious precisely because it is a matter of slow-paced, formal gesture and movement rather than mere words, now devalued as a currency through remarks such as Beatrice's rebuke to all the men present in the church scene: 'manhood is melted into curtsies, valour into compliment, and men are only turned into tongue, and trim ones too' (IV.1.313–15).

The conscious reworking of earlier elements of the play continues throughout Act V. Scene 4 revisits both the masked ball scene and the church scene together, in order to complete the journey from suspicion to faith. It echoes and transforms aspects of both those earlier scenes, and further constructs a benign theatricality. As in the church scene, the backstage preparations are shown first. Strikingly, the play continues to take risks, as the same old joking about the savage bull and horns is rerun for the third time between Don Pedro, Claudio and Benedick:

DON PEDRO
　Good morrow, Benedick. Why, what's the matter,
　That you have such a February face,
　So full of frost, of storm and cloudiness?

CLAUDIO

   I think he thinks upon the savage bull.

   Tush, fear not, man, we'll tip thy horns with gold,

   And all Europa shall rejoice at thee,

   As once Europa did at lusty Jove,

   When he would play the noble beast in love.

BENEDICK

   Bull Jove, sir, had an amiable low;

   And some such strange bull leaped your father's cow,

   And got a calf in that same noble feat

   Much like to you, for you have just his bleat. (V.4.40–51)

Claudio's joke continues the running thread of cuckold jokes and represents the third reference to 'the savage bull' (see also I.1.241–7 and V.1.174–7 above). He ironically 'reassures' Benedick about marriage by promising to make cuckoldry pleasurable (tip his horns with gold) as a condition licensing Benedick to take his own pleasure of 'all Europa' (V.4.45; the pun links Europe with the classical figure of Europa who was raped by Jove in the form of a bull). Benedick's response is reminiscent of Leonato's earlier joke in response to Don Pedro's enquiry as to whether Hero is his daughter ('Her mother hath many times told me so') and insults Claudio with the slur of bastardy, the logical consequence of sexual infidelity. The strength of both these slurs, unfaithfulness and bastardy, brings the unspoken taboo represented by Don John into focus and insists indirectly on the bastard's opposition to marriage in such a society as inevitable rather than random.

   The same groupings as in the wedding scene reappear, the Friar presiding, but with this difference: that the ladies from the group enter masked. This puts it in dialogue with the ball scene, where the men enter as a masked group. Where, in the ball scene, the masks made it possible to interact indirectly, withholding feeling and playing with postures, here the masks are the measure of faith, since Claudio must take Hero's hand and swear to marry her before he sees her face; and it is this act of faith that allows Hero to unmask and reveal herself: 'And when I lived, I was your other wife; | And when you loved, you were my other husband' (V.4.60–61). For Beatrice and Benedick too, the scene reworks and transforms their encounter at the ball. Following Hero's unmasking here, Benedick interrupts the movement towards fulfilling the rites of Hero's wedding in the chapel:

BENEDICK
  Soft and fair, Friar. Which is Beatrice?
BEATRICE (*unmasking*)
  I answer to that name. What is your will? (72–3)

The moment compares directly and antithetically with Benedick's refusal to acknowledge his identity to Beatrice at the ball:

BEATRICE Will you not tell me who told you so?
BENEDICK No, you shall pardon me.
BEATRICE Nor will you not tell me who you are?
BENEDICK Not now (II.1.111–14);

and the sexual pun inherent in Beatrice's use of 'will' (meaning also 'desire') reprises the way in which her desire slipped out in that previous encounter: 'I would he had boarded me' (128–9). There is a brief return to verbal fencing in the dialogue that follows on Beatrice's open unmasking in this final scene, in which both seek to underplay their feeling for each other as they discover the trick played on them, but, in a wry glance at more romantic plots, the sonnets they have written belie their attempts to backtrack on love: 'A miracle! Here's our own hands against our hearts' (Benedick, V.4.91–2).

The long-awaited kiss puts an end to words and with it to any possible misreading of this sign:

BENEDICK (*kissing her*) Peace! I will stop your mouth (97)

(though there is a nice irony about the fact that the signs were seemingly misread by an early compositor of the play, who attributed this line to Leonato rather than Benedick). The line, and perhaps too the gesture it scripts, is reminiscent of the moment at the end of the masque scene when Beatrice tells Hero how to respond to Claudio's betrothal of himself: 'Speak, cousin; or, if you cannot, stop his mouth with a kiss, and let not him speak neither' (II.1.286–7). In both scenes the kiss both represses and satisfies, but what it represses is not desire, which is at least partly satisfied, but fickle, slippery words. This is self-evidently the point that a play dealing so much in repressed desire and misread signs needs to reach for completeness. 'Stopping' is both cutting off and completing. The word as well as the action is also plain and direct: simultaneously bald, bold, rough and romantic. It brings together realism and idealism in a way that makes perfect sense for two lovers who can respectively 'see yet without spectacles' (Benedick, I.1.177) and 'see a church by daylight' (Beatrice, II.1.73–4). Marriage for this couple, these lines seem to emphasize, is not about fashion, glitter and getting the look right; they are not concerned, as Margaret and Hero are, with finding a wedding gown of 'cloth o'gold, and cuts, and laced with silver, set with pearls, down-sleeves, side-sleeves, and skirts, round underborne with a bluish tinsel', to outstrip the Duchess of Milan's (III.4.18–20). Benedick's conclusion, as offered in response to Don Pedro's mockery following this kiss, encapsulates a hard-headed but, it is implied, tougher and more resistant attitude to marriage than that so easily toppled in the Hero–Claudio plot:

DON PEDRO How dost thou, Benedick the married man?
BENEDICK I'll tell thee what, Prince; a college of wit-crackers cannot flout me out of my humour. Dost thou think I care for a satire or an epigram? No: if a man will be beaten with brains, 'a shall wear nothing handsome about him. In brief, since I do purpose to marry, I will think nothing to any purpose that the world can say against it; and therefore never flout at me for what I have said against it; for man is a giddy thing, and this is my conclusion. (V.4.98–107)

The imagery of clothes picks up on the superficial concern for fashion that has run through the play, and rejects it in rejecting the wearing of anything handsome. And yet in concluding as he does, Benedick does not exclude himself from the the general 'giddiness' of humanity. All acknowledge some frailty; and the last joke of the play returns to the favourite motif of 'horn' (underlining it with the obvious sexual pun on 'staff'): 'There is no staff more reverend than one tipped with horn' (121–2). The horn joke, of course, though its connotations of cuckoldry are undeniable when the horns are plural, can always claim to be only or primarily a reference to straightforward sexual desire, and performance can point the emphasis one way or another.

The play closes with a reminder of both theatricality and indirectness, as the arrival of a messenger recalls the play's opening, and the clarity of that circular structure reminds us that this is, after all, not human life, but carefully shaped theatre. The closing dance is a highly self-conscious piece of staging that reminds the audience above all that this play, though it has included moments that set it apart from other comedies, including other Shakespearian comedies, here aligns itself with theatrical comic tradition in fulfilling the audience's desire for closure and happy ending. Even Don John's punishment is postponed while Benedick instructs the pipers to strike up for the dance, and the call for music satisfyingly reiterates the thread of music, song, masque and dance that has run through the play in counterpoint with its verbal fireworks but relative absence of verbal music. Thus a highly theatrical play closes with a predictable happy ending that fulfils expectation, and at the same time reminds the audience that it is only in theatrical fairyland that so much pain and brutality can finally be dismissed as much ado about nothing.

Janette Dillon

The Play in Performance

Much Ado About Nothing has long been a popular favourite of the Shakespearian repertoire. It was the play chosen for the opening of the Shakespeare Memorial Theatre in Stratford in 1879, with Helen Faucit and Barry Sullivan in the roles of Beatrice and Benedick, and has remained in regular performance ever since. But despite evidence of the play's early popularity (see Introduction, p. xxi), only one specific performance is documented in Shakespeare's lifetime: the court performance in 1613 as part of the festivities for the marriage between the Princess Elizabeth, daughter of James I, and the Elector Palatine. Little is known about the play's earliest productions, but we have the evidence of speech headings in the first Quarto to show that Dogberry was first played by the famous comic actor Will Kemp. Kemp, who left the Chamberlain's Men in 1599, was a clown in the old tradition of improvisation and comic gags, known for his jigs (short, often bawdy, afterpieces with song and dance), and possibly one of the performers who prompted Shakespeare to write Hamlet's well-known speech rebuking clowns who 'speak . . . more than is set down for them' (III.2.38). It is likely therefore that much of the humour of early performances of the play lay beyond the script in the physical and improvisational comedy of its clowns.

As Leonard Digges's poem shows, however (see Introduction, pp. xxi–xxii), Beatrice and Benedick, though technically part of the subplot of the play, clearly seized and dominated the imaginations of early spectators as they continue to do now. Besides the evidence of Digges, a payment list for the wedding of 1613 refers to the play as 'Benedicte and Betteris'; and Charles I, who may have first seen the play performed at his sister's wedding, also famously wrote 'Benedik and Betrice' next to the title of the play in his copy of the second Folio edition of 1632. Berlioz's opera of 1862 continues the tradition of naming the work after these two characters. The play effectively disappeared from the Restoration stage, in so far as William Davenant's adaptation, *The Law Against Lovers* (1662), combined the play with *Measure for Measure*. Shakespeare's version, however, was revived in 1721 and became a particular favourite from 1748 to 1776, while David Garrick played Benedick, which he did every year until his retirement. One problem, of course, about having a great actor in the part of Benedick, is finding a Beatrice to match. The pairing can easily become a competitive one, as indeed the text partly scripts it to be. Ways of playing that pairing have changed considerably since Garrick's time, most notably, in recent times, with the tendency to cast older actors as Beatrice and Benedick. Whereas Garrick grew old naturally in the role, as star actors, retaining their parts over many years, often did at that time, productions since the 1970s have frequently made a conscious choice to cast Beatrice and Benedick as more mature, expanding on the play's hints that their relationship goes back some time (see Introduction, p. xxxv) and perhaps also seeking to motivate their reluctance to love. Pairings of older actors in the roles have included Elizabeth Spriggs and Derek Godfrey in 1971,

Judi Dench and Donald Sinden in 1976, Felicity Kendal
and Alan Bates in 1989 and Harriet Walter and Nicholas
Le Prevost in 2002. This casting highlights the contrast
between Beatrice and Benedick and Hero and Claudio,
always cast as young, and can help to build up a context
of youthful naivety and idealism to motivate Claudio's
impulsive rejection of Hero. Its risk, however, is a
reduction of sexual tension. As one reviewer noted of
the Spriggs–Godfrey production, this Beatrice and
Benedick were more likely to become 'a popular party-
going host and hostess' than to make love (Penny Gay,
As She Likes It).

   Looking for motivation, however, has been a characteristic of twentieth-century productions since the
dissemination of Stanislavski's methods of actor-training,
with his emphasis on building characters (though a
tendency to psychologize performance had been
increasing before Stanislavski, since at least the early nineteenth century). Motivating the 'merry war' between
Beatrice and Benedick has involved looking particularly
hard at their past. Maggie Steed, playing opposite Clive
Merrison in Di Trevis's production of the play at Stratford
in 1988, for example, talked about the tyranny of the
relentless clowning that seems to drive Beatrice's speech
rhythms: 'Repeatedly, she uses a rhythm almost characteristic of the stand-up comic – setting up an idea,
expanding on it, and then capping it, throwing it away.'
She goes on to describe how, in rehearsing the famous
lines about Beatrice's birth, 'my mother cried; but then
there was a star danced, and under that was I born'
(II.1.309–10), she found herself saying 'my mother died'
and was moved to tears. The moment, as Steed describes
it, was 'terribly important . . . it opened a chink into her
feelings and I knew that I had to find a way to let that

truth be seen for a moment and covered again' ('Beatrice in *Much Ado About Nothing*'). (John Cox's commentary on this line in his edition of the play gives a brief summary of the way actresses since Ellen Terry have delivered the line.)

Such a way of thinking about a dramatic character would have been totally alien from Shakespeare's time until at least the end of the eighteenth century, though a tendency to think about Beatrice as a woman who had experienced sorrow seems to have begun with Helen Faucit, who first played the role in 1836. Before that, interpreting Beatrice was not only, or even mainly, a matter of acting style, but of conventional hierarchies within the theatre. While Garrick played the part of Benedick, for example, it was unthinkable for any Beatrice to consider upstaging him, though some of the Beatrices who played opposite him (notably Frances Abington) were acclaimed in the role. And Garrick's influence lingered on: more than twenty years after Garrick's death, Dorothea Jordan, who came to the part in 1797 and was lauded as one of the great Beatrices of her time, described the role as 'a very easy quiet part'. As actor-managers began to star in the role of Benedick in the eighteenth and nineteenth centuries, the tendency to inflate Benedick's presence at the expense of Beatrice's integrity and credibility grew more dominant and it became the custom to rewrite Shakespeare in order to create 'curtain-lines', climactic moments that would elicit spontaneous applause.

The church scene was and is a central crux in performance. Beatrice's potentially most scene-stealing line is spoken in response to Benedick's light-hearted, even ironic adoption of the lover's pose in this scene, where they first admit their love to each other: 'Come, bid me do anything for thee' (IV.1.284). Her reply – 'Kill

Claudio' – punctures his playfulness with its terse and chilling seriousness. Eighteenth- and nineteenth-century theatre performance texts contained wholesale rewritings of this sequence aimed at shifting the weight of seriousness towards Benedick. John Philip Kemble, playing Benedick, had inserted the following dialogue after Beatrice's 'Kill Claudio' by 1788:

Ben. Enough; I am engaged; I'll challenge him.
Bea. Will you?
Ben. Upon my soul, I will . . . I'll kiss your hand, and so leave you . . . By this hand, Claudio shall render me a dear account.
Bea. You'll be sure to challenge him.
Ben. By those bright eyes, I will. [*going LH*]
Bea. My dear friend – kiss my hand again.
Ben. As you hear of me, so think of me. Go, comfort your cousin:– I must say, she is dead:– and so, farewell. [*Both going.*]
Bea. Benedick, – kill him, kill him, if you can.
Ben. As sure as he is alive, I will.
                [*Exeunt Ben. L. Bea. R.*]

Even more laughable, to modern ears, is the variation of this adaptation acted by Walter Lacy in the part of Benedick in 1859:

BENEDICK I will challenge him.
BEATRICE And fight him?
BENEDICK Fight him!
BEATRICE Kill him?
BENEDICK Kill him!
BEATRICE Dead?
BENEDICK Dead!

Ellen Terry describes the struggle to overturn this tradition of inflating the star male role as late as 1882. For one battle won, another was lost. Henry Irving, manager of the Lyceum and starring as Benedick, engaged Lacy, 'an actor of the old school', to coach her, she says, in 'some traditional "business" which seemed to me so preposterous that I could hardly believe he really meant me to adopt it' (*Four Lectures*). One piece of 'business' that especially offended Terry involved having Beatrice 'shoo' Benedick away from Hero when he goes to her aid after she has fainted following Claudio's accusation in the church, as a way of demonstrating her supposed jealousy when he goes to touch another woman. 'Oh, nonsense, Mr Lacy' was Terry's response to these instructions. Lacy's defence, Terry reports, was that 'it's always been done . . . and it always gets a laugh'. Terry won the run-in with Lacy, but lost to Irving, despite tears and pleading, over the traditional 'Kiss my hand again' gag at the end of the scene. As she reflected bitterly, in considering whether to throw up the part, 'for one thing I did not like doing at the Lyceum, there would probably be a hundred things I should dislike doing in another theatre. So I agreed to do what Henry wished, under protest.'

Nowadays actors worry that even the shock of the single line 'Kill Claudio' may raise a laugh, and the question of how to avoid it is a significant element informing decisions about how to play it. Janet Suzman and Alan Howard got a laugh in a Stratford production of 1969 when they broke the orderly formality and restraint of their delivery up to that point by shouting out 'Kill Claudio' – 'Ha! Not for the wide world'. Not surprisingly, they toned down their delivery when the production moved to the Aldwych. Earlier ways of playing this

exchange were notably more comic, sentimental or melo-
dramatic, according to the customs of the time, than is
commonly the case now. Garrick's performance of this
extract was noted as one of the most entertaining
sequences of the play; Miss Brunton, playing at Covent
Garden in 1817, giggled repeatedly between bursts of
indignation; Louisa Nisbett, in 1843, threw her arms
around Benedick and broke into sobs; Irving and Terry
indulged in prolonged kissing and embracing. John
Gielgud's performance, playing with Diana Wynyard in
1952 and with Peggy Ashcroft in 1950 and 1955, has been
most praised among modern performances for its deli-
cacy, while Judi Dench and Donald Sinden in John
Barton's Stratford production of 1976 achieved a
compelling intensity that contrasted with the brittle
brightness of their earlier interchanges.

The play has been set in numerous locations but the
Shakespearian setting of Messina has led to many recent
productions adopting a sunny, Sicilian carelessness which
is especially emphatic in Kenneth Branagh's filmed
version of 1993; and Sicily is also the setting for the BBC
version of 1984. When sets first became really detailed
and lavish in the nineteenth century, the play's
Mediterranean setting offered an inviting opportunity to
create warmth and exoticism. Charles Kean's final production of the 1858 season opened with a rising moon slowly
lighting up the elegant houses, harbour and sea. Greg
Doran's 2002 production for the Royal Shakespeare
Company emphasized the dark side as well as the sunlight
of stereotypical Sicily, drawing in the programme notes
on Mafioso ideas of manliness to explain the play's highly
developed sense of male honour. The Italian director
Franco Zeffirelli, by contrast, designed and directed a
production at the National Theatre in 1965 which

enclosed the acting space within hessian flats, hung the proscenium arch with strings of lights and invoked the Mafia only comically through the performance of Derek Jacobi as Don John, dressed in a double-breasted suit and eating Rice Krispies. Productions seeking to transpose the play to locations and historical moments that have elicited different equivalences have included Douglas Seale's operetta-style Italy (1958), J. J. Antoon's pre-First World War, small-town America (1972), John Barton's British Raj (1976) and Terence Knapp's nineteenth-century Meiji Japan, in a Tokyo production (1975, 1977).

Stanislavski, impressed by a reconstructed medieval castle on a visit to Turin, and looking for a play that might serve as a vehicle for such a set, decided that his ideas 'could best be crammed into *Much Ado About Nothing*', produced in 1897 (Joyce Vining Morgan, *Stanislavski's Encounter with Shakespeare*). Other landmark set designs eschewed a representational approach ahead of their time. Edward Gordon Craig, Ellen Terry's son, designed and directed a production at the Lyceum in 1903 (his only Shakespeare production in his native country) that used spare effects of light and texture (pillars painted on curtains, a wickerwork garden) in place of scenic realism. Johnston Forbes-Robertson's painting of Irving's highly elaborate church interior shows the kind of context against which Craig's stark effects seemed so shocking. In America Robert Edmond Jones, believing that stage design 'should be addressed to [the] eye of the mind' rather than 'a thing to look at in itself', designed an austere chiaroscuro production in 1925 that emphasized mood changes through changes in lighting (*The Dramatic Imagination*).

Two last issues for consideration here are strongly

linked to decisions about setting and overall ambience:
the characterization of Don John and the ending of the
play. Sheldon Zitner has described Don John as 'necessary but not important' (*Much Ado About Nothing*), by
which he means that the role is primarily a plot device;
and in the Introduction to this edition I have argued
similarly that there is a narrative and symbolic logic to
the role of the bastard that overrides any psychological
considerations. But the drive towards motivation, as I
have suggested above in this section on performance,
scarcely knows how to make space for characters who
are not characterful and has to find some way of making
the part sit comfortably within an otherwise predominantly realist mode. The tendency to give the part to a
notable star, such as Derek Jacobi, Richard Pasco or Ian
Richardson, is evidence of a feeling that the role needs
to be given special attention and development. The
stutter of Richardson's Don John, for example, gave a
special prominence and psychological underpinning to
his exclusion from the witty banter of the central protagonists. Perhaps only the Prospect Theatre's 1970
production, with its decision to have Don John shot by
Don Pedro just before the command to merriment that
closes the play, 'Strike up, pipers', allowed for a plot-
driven character, paradoxically by completely rewriting
the plot.

The ending has been subject to rewriting over an
extended period. An ending represents, after all, the
clearest opportunity for a curtain-line; and it was one that
earlier Benedicks could not resist. Kemble rearranged the
sequence of the ending to allow Benedick to repeat the
toothache joke to Don Pedro and to make his final horn
joke the closing couplet of the play:

Got the tooth-ake! – Get thee a wife; and all will be well.
  – Nay, laugh not, laugh not:–
Your gibes and mockeries I laugh to scorn;
No staff more reverend, than one tipp'd with horn.

The closing call for music, as scripted by Shakespeare, however, focuses on the ensemble rather than the star, and on collective celebration rather than individual wit. In a carefree, sun-soaked setting this can lead to an escape into 'hey nonny nonsense'(Courtney Lehmann, '*Much Ado About Nothing*: Shakespeare, Branagh and the "National-Popular" in the Age of Multinational Capital', *Textual Practice* 12 (1998)); but Benedick's last lines before the call for music, in which he responds to news of Don John's escape and capture, are double-edged, simultaneously dismissing and summoning dark thoughts of retribution: 'Think not on him till tomorrow; I'll devise thee brave punishments for him.' The play leavens its festivity with thoughts of what is to follow, allowing for a more compromised and ambiguous expression of harmony.

                                                    Janette Dillon

Further Reading

There has been much less critical ado about *Much Ado* than about the other two Shakespearian comedies to which it is closest in time, *As You Like It* and *Twelfth Night*. Two full-length studies of the play, by J. R. Mulryne (*Shakespeare: 'Much Ado About Nothing'*, 1965) and Roger Sales (*'Much Ado About Nothing': A Critical Study*, 1987), introduce it in a lively and stimulating way, with Mulryne paying pioneering attention to the visual effects of the play in performance and Sales adding much relevant contextual material. John Russell Brown's Casebook collection (1979) brings together some very useful material from across the full chronological range of criticism, including some of Samuel Johnson's comments (quoted in the Introduction to this volume) and a variety of responses to the play in performance across the years; and Penny Gay's study of twentieth-century performances of female Shakespearian parts (*As She Likes It: Shakespeare's Unruly Women*, 1994) takes the study of the play in the theatre closer to the present day. Brown's collection includes Barbara Everett's influential early essay (first published in 1961), in which, comparing the play with Shakespeare's other comedies, she notes its lack of a sunlit wood, a heroine in hose or a play within a play, and describes it, by contrast, as a play for 'working-days' rather than holidays. A later critical collection by Linda Cookson and Bryan Loughrey (*Critical Essays on 'Much Ado About Nothing'*, 1989) brings together an excellent group of short and pithy essays showing some of the directions in which criticism has developed in the decade since Russell Brown's collection.

Charles Prouty's book-length study of the play's sources (*The Sources of 'Much Ado About Nothing'*, 1950) argues strongly that Shakespeare's alterations make his play into a study of arranged marriage within which Claudio should be seen as a realist, not a romantic lover. Geoffrey Bullough's aim in his monumental *Narrative and Dramatic Sources of Shakespeare* (1957–75; sources for *Much Ado* are in vol. II) is primarily to make the relevant sources available to the reader, but for him the most remarkable feature of Shakespeare's version is his omission of the scene in which the lover sees his supposed rival at his lady's window, an omission aimed, Bullough argues, at focusing attention on 'hearsay and false report' as a major theme. Brean Hammond and Leo Salingar move this argument beyond the thematic in rather different ways, Hammond (in Cookson and Loughrey (eds.), above) arguing that the very point of the deception is its thinness, which reveals Messina as a society already riddled with distrust, while Salingar ('Borachio's Indiscretion: Some Noting about *Much Ado*', in *The Italian World of English Renaissance Drama*, ed. Michele Marrapodi, 1998) argues that the play, rather than focusing on slander and masquerade, as do its sources, becomes an exploration of social communication itself.

For several critics the issues of distrust and communication are nuanced in a gendered way in this play, and a focus on gender issues has been a strong element in responses to *Much Ado* since at least the eighteenth century. Francis Gentleman's notes to the Bell's Plays edition of 1774 reprimand the unseemliness of Beatrice's wit: 'Beatrice rather trespasses on virgin decency; archness and modesty are no ways incompatible; therefore it is a pity the author should have suffered this pleasant girl to exceed decorum.' Henrietta Palmer, writing in 1859, remarks drily that Beatrice proves in her own person 'that the "fast" woman is by no means a modern "institution"' (Ann Thompson and Sasha Roberts, *Women Reading Shakespeare 1660–1900*, 1997). Some of these early writers excused Beatrice's frankness on the grounds that Elizabethan social decorum had allowed women much greater freedom than was subsequently the case, and Mary Augusta Scott, in an essay of 1901 ('*The Book of the Courtyer*: A Possible Source of Benedick and Beatrice', *PMLA* 16), made the case for Beatrice as specifically modelled on Castiglione's representation of Lady Emilia Pia in *The Book of the Courtier* (translated into English in 1561).

Ellen Terry's performance in the role at the end of the nineteenth century marked the start of a more feminist celebration of Beatrice (see 'The Play in Performance'), though a more conservative line of criticism condemned her as a 'tartar' and an 'odious woman' (Thomas Campbell, quoted in the Cambridge edition of the play, ed. Arthur Quiller-Couch and John Dover Wilson, 1953). Given the intense interest in the Elizabethan tradition of the boy-actor in recent decades, however, and the degree to which this has dominated criticism of so much Renaissance drama, including especially Shakespeare's comedies, *Much Ado*'s general absence from such discussions is striking. Beatrice and Hero, in their failure to disguise as males, and in their contrasting modes of femaleness, clearly do not problematize gender in similar

ways to Rosalind or Viola. Gender-based analyses of the
play tend to point firmly in the essentialist direction of
clear-cut differences between men and women, not
towards gender as in any way blurred or socially
performed. Barbara Everett (1961) proposed that this was
the first of Shakespeare's plays to treat the clash of male
and female worlds seriously, and Sherman Hawkins
(1967) notes the parallelism between scenes with men and
scenes with women in the play (both reprinted in Russell
Brown's Casebook). Janice Hays ('"Those Soft and
Delicate Desires": *Much Ado* and the Distrust of Women',
in *The Woman's Part: Feminist Criticism of Shakespeare*,
ed. C. Lenz et al., 1980) further identified the play as one
of Shakespeare's earliest dramatizations of a motif that
was to be repeated: the sexual distrust of a woman,
followed by her testing and vindication. Carol Cook,
writing in 1986 ('The Sign and Semblance of Her
Honour: Reading Gender Difference in *Much Ado About
Nothing*', *PMLA* 101), sees both these critics as giving
false moral closure to the play by a privileging of the
feminine. She offers a reading that resists the play's movement towards 'ritual transcendence', drawing attention,
via Sigmund Freud, to Shakespeare's conscious use of
Dogberry to expose the crux that the main plot seeks to
avoid confronting: Claudio's failure to be transformed
by Hero's seeming death. Harry Berger (*Making Trifles
of Terrors*, 1997) points to the way Hero's death brings
the members of the 'Men's Club' of Messina together:
while Hero's suspected betrayal of Claudio is 'a heinous
crime against the whole Men's Club, Claudio and the
Prince find themselves guilty only of a pardonable error
in judgment, a position they coolly maintain in the face
of Hero's announced death'.

   The repeated reference to cuckoldry and the function

of jokes in the play are also important to readings by
Carol Neely (*Broken Nuptials in Shakespeare's Plays*, 1985)
and Michael Mangan (*A Preface to Shakespeare's Comedies
1594–1603*, 1996). Neely's study takes its starting point
from Leo Salingar's analysis of this plot-structure as
widespread in Shakespeare's comedies and as a funda-
mental motive regularly underpinning his alterations to
sources across a number of plays (*Shakespeare and the
Traditions of Comedy*, 1974), while Mangan sees Beatrice
and Benedick representing a cynical view of love and
marriage against an idealistic courtly view, represented
by Claudio and Hero.

A critical focus on masquing and masquerade, evident
in several of the pieces cited above, brings together the
structural interest in form and symmetry with the thematic
identification of deceit. Harold Jenkins's essay on the ball
scene (in *Shakespeare: Text, Language, Criticism*, ed. B.
Fabian and K. Tetzeli von Rosador, 1987) enumerates the
play's multiple symmetries with clarity and elegance,
besides showing how the shape of the betrothal masque
both foreshadows the shape of the wedding scene and
enacts the larger pattern of marriage itself. The focus on
masque links too with a focus on theatricality itself, most
notably taken up by Jean Howard ('Renaissance Anti-
theatricality and the Politics of Gender and Rank in *Much
Ado About Nothing*', in *Shakespeare Reproduced*, ed. J. E.
Howard and M. F. O'Connor, 1987) within the context
of the antitheatrical writings of the period. The formalism
of its dramaturgy, however, can be shown to be part of
what Alexander Leggatt calls a 'mixture of dramatic
idiom' (*Shakespeare's Comedy of Love*, 1974), an interplay between formalism and naturalism that makes the
experience of the play very changeable from moment to
moment. And this interplay of dramatic modes goes hand

in hand with what Salingar (in *The Italian World*, above) calls 'unexpected relations between pathos and gaiety'. Barbara Everett's 1994 revisiting of the play ('*Much Ado About Nothing*: The Unsociable Comedy', in *English Comedy*, ed. Michael Cordner, Peter Holland and John Kerrigan) emends a reading of Leonato's speech at the start of Act V, scene 1 to include the phrase 'sorrow's wag', a concept which she then explores as emblematic of the play's concern to bring a comical element in, where we least expect it, to the experience of sorrow, thereby making us 'think very hard indeed about this quality of the "passionate" in human beings'. It is a conclusion, as the Introduction here shows, that goes back to Samuel Johnson's argument that we should take note of the looseness of generic concepts at the time Shakespeare was writing.

There are three other major editions of *Much Ado*: the Oxford edition, edited by Sheldon Zitner (1993); the New Cambridge, by F. H. Mares (1988); and the Arden edition by A. R. Humphreys (1981). Zitner's introduction is the fullest and includes an excellent section on the history of the play in performance. John F. Cox's performance-based edition for the Cambridge Shakespeare in Production series (1997) supplies a richly detailed context of performance for the play through line-by-line commentary as well as an introductory overview. A list of reading relating to the Play in Performance follows.

Cox, J. F., 'The Stage Representation of the "Kill Claudio" Sequence in *Much Ado About Nothing*', *Shakespeare Survey 23* (1979), pp. 27–36.

Cox, J. F. (ed.), *Much Ado About Nothing*, Shakespeare in Production (1997).

Gay, Penny, *As She Likes It: Shakespeare's Unruly Women* (1994).

Jones, Robert Edmond, *The Dramatic Imagination: Reflections and Speculations on the Art of the Theatre* (1941).

Mason, Pamela, *Much Ado About Nothing* (1992).

Morgan, Joyce Vining, *Stanislavski's Encounter with Shakespeare: The Evolution of a Method* (1984).

Shattuck, Charles H. (ed.), *John Philip Kemble's Promptbooks* (1974).

Speaight, Robert, *Shakespeare on the Stage: An Illustrated History of Shakespearian Performance* (1973).

Steed, Maggie, 'Beatrice in *Much Ado About Nothing*', in *Players of Shakespeare 3*, ed. Russell Jackson and Robert Smallwood (1993).

Terry, Ellen, *Four Lectures on Shakespeare*, ed. Christopher St John (1932).

Trewin, J. C., *Shakespeare on the English Stage, 1900–1964: A Survey of Productions* (1964).

Zitner, Sheldon (ed.), *Much Ado About Nothing*, Oxford edition (1993).

MUCH ADO ABOUT NOTHING

The Characters in the Play

DON PEDRO, Prince of Arragon
BENEDICK, of Padua ⎫ young lords, companions of
CLAUDIO, of Florence ⎭ Don Pedro
DON JOHN, Don Pedro's bastard brother
BORACHIO ⎫
CONRADE ⎭ followers of Don John
LEONATO, Governor of Messina
ANTONIO, his brother, an old man
BALTHASAR, a singer
FRIAR Francis, a priest

HERO, Leonato's daughter
MARGARET ⎫
URSULA ⎭ attendants on Hero
BEATRICE, an orphan, Leonato's niece

DOGBERRY, the Constable in charge of the Watch
VERGES, the Headborough, Dogberry's partner in authority
A SEXTON, and several WATCHMEN, under Dogberry's
   authority

MESSENGERS
A BOY, servant to Benedick
Antonio's son
LORD
Attendants and musicians in Leonato's household

*Enter Leonato, Governor of Messina, Hero, his
daughter, Beatrice, his niece, with a Messenger*

LEONATO I learn in this letter that Don Pedro of Arragon
comes this night to Messina.

MESSENGER He is very near by this; he was not three
leagues off when I left him.

LEONATO How many gentlemen have you lost in this
action?

MESSENGER But few of any sort, and none of name.

LEONATO A victory is twice itself when the achiever brings
home full numbers. I find here that Don Pedro hath
bestowed much honour on a young Florentine called   10
Claudio.

MESSENGER Much deserved on his part and equally remembered by Don Pedro. He hath borne himself beyond the promise of his age, doing, in the figure of a
lamb, the feats of a lion; he hath indeed better bettered
expectation than you must expect of me to tell you how.

LEONATO He hath an uncle here in Messina will be very
much glad of it.

MESSENGER I have already delivered him letters, and
there appears much joy in him; even so much that joy   20
could not show itself modest enough without a badge of
bitterness.

LEONATO Did he break out into tears?

MESSENGER In great measure.

LEONATO A kind overflow of kindness; there are no faces
    truer than those that are so washed. How much better is
    it to weep at joy than to joy at weeping!

BEATRICE I pray you, is Signor Mountanto returned from
    the wars, or no?

30 MESSENGER I know none of that name, lady; there was
    none such in the army of any sort.

LEONATO What is he that you ask for, niece?

HERO My cousin means Signor Benedick of Padua.

MESSENGER O, he's returned, and as pleasant as ever he
    was.

BEATRICE He set up his bills here in Messina, and chal-
    lenged Cupid at the flight; and my uncle's fool, reading
    the challenge, subscribed for Cupid, and challenged him
    at the bird-bolt. I pray you, how many hath he killed and
40 eaten in these wars? But how many hath he killed? For
    indeed, I promised to eat all of his killing.

LEONATO Faith, niece, you tax Signor Benedick too much;
    but he'll be meet with you, I doubt it not.

MESSENGER He hath done good service, lady, in these
    wars.

BEATRICE You had musty victual, and he hath holp to eat
    it; he is a very valiant trencher-man, he hath an excel-
    lent stomach.

MESSENGER And a good soldier too, lady.

50 BEATRICE And a good soldier to a lady. But what is he to a
    lord?

MESSENGER A lord to a lord, a man to a man, stuffed with
    all honourable virtues.

BEATRICE It is so, indeed; he is no less than a stuffed man;
    but for the stuffing – well, we are all mortal.

LEONATO You must not, sir, mistake my niece. There is a

kind of merry war betwixt Signor Benedick and her;
they never meet but there's a skirmish of wit between
them.

BEATRICE Alas, he gets nothing by that. In our last con-   60
flict four of his five wits went halting off, and now is the
whole man governed with one; so that if he have wit
enough to keep himself warm, let him bear it for a
difference between himself and his horse; for it is all the
wealth that he hath left, to be known a reasonable creature. Who is his companion now? He hath every month
a new sworn brother.

MESSENGER Is't possible?

BEATRICE Very easily possible: he wears his faith but as
the fashion of his hat; it ever changes with the next   70
block.

MESSENGER I see, lady, the gentleman is not in your books.

BEATRICE No; an he were, I would burn my study. But,
I pray you, who is his companion? Is there no young
squarer now that will make a voyage with him to the
devil?

MESSENGER He is most in the company of the right noble
Claudio.

BEATRICE O Lord, he will hang upon him like a disease.
He is sooner caught than the pestilence, and the taker   80
runs presently mad. God help the noble Claudio! If he
have caught the Benedick, it will cost him a thousand
pound ere 'a be cured.

MESSENGER I will hold friends with you, lady.

BEATRICE Do, good friend.

LEONATO You will never run mad, niece.

BEATRICE No, not till a hot January.

MESSENGER Don Pedro is approached.

Enter Don Pedro, Claudio, Benedick, Balthasar, and
Don John the Bastard

DON PEDRO Good Signor Leonato, are you come to meet
90   your trouble? The fashion of the world is to avoid cost,
        and you encounter it.

LEONATO Never came trouble to my house in the likeness
        of your grace; for trouble being gone, comfort should
        remain; but when you depart from me sorrow abides,
        and happiness takes his leave.

DON PEDRO You embrace your charge too willingly. I
        think this is your daughter.

LEONATO Her mother hath many times told me so.

BENEDICK Were you in doubt, sir, that you asked her?

100   LEONATO Signor Benedick, no; for then were you a child.

DON PEDRO You have it full, Benedick; we may guess by
        this what you are, being a man. Truly, the lady fathers
        herself. Be happy, lady; for you are like an honourable
        father.

BENEDICK If Signor Leonato be her father, she would not
        have his head on her shoulders for all Messina, as like
        him as she is.

BEATRICE I wonder that you will still be talking, Signor
        Benedick; nobody marks you.

110   BENEDICK What, my dear Lady Disdain! Are you yet
        living?

BEATRICE Is it possible disdain should die while she hath
        such meet food to feed it as Signor Benedick? Courtesy
        itself must convert to disdain, if you come in her
        presence.

BENEDICK Then is courtesy a turncoat. But it is certain I
        am loved of all ladies, only you excepted; and I would
        I could find in my heart that I had not a hard heart, for,
        truly, I love none.

120   BEATRICE A dear happiness to women; they would else
        have been troubled with a pernicious suitor! I thank
        God and my cold blood, I am of your humour for that;

I had rather hear my dog bark at a crow than a man swear
he loves me.

BENEDICK God keep your ladyship still in that mind!
So some gentleman or other shall 'scape a predestinate
scratched face.

BEATRICE Scratching could not make it worse, an 'twere
such a face as yours were.

BENEDICK Well, you are a rare parrot-teacher.   130

BEATRICE A bird of my tongue is better than a beast of
yours.

BENEDICK I would my horse had the speed of your tongue,
and so good a continuer. But keep your way a' God's
name, I have done.

BEATRICE You always end with a jade's trick; I know you
of old.

DON PEDRO That is the sum of all, Leonato. Signor
Claudio and Signor Benedick, my dear friend Leonato
hath invited you all. I tell him we shall stay here at the   140
least a month, and he heartily prays some occasion may
detain us longer. I dare swear he is no hypocrite, but
prays from his heart.

LEONATO If you swear, my lord, you shall not be for-
sworn. (*To Don John*) Let me bid you welcome, my
lord, being reconciled to the Prince your brother. I owe
you all duty.

DON JOHN I thank you. I am not of many words, but I
thank you.

LEONATO Please it your grace lead on?   150

DON PEDRO Your hand, Leonato; we will go together.
                     Exeunt all except Benedick and Claudio

CLAUDIO Benedick, didst thou note the daughter of Signor
Leonato?

BENEDICK I noted her not, but I looked on her.

CLAUDIO Is she not a modest young lady?

BENEDICK Do you question me as an honest man should do, for my simple true judgement? Or would you have me speak after my custom, as being a professed tyrant to their sex?

160 CLAUDIO No, I pray thee speak in sober judgement.

BENEDICK Why, i'faith, methinks she's too low for a high praise, too brown for a fair praise, and too little for a great praise; only this commendation I can afford her, that were she other than she is, she were unhandsome; and being no other but as she is, I do not like her.

CLAUDIO Thou thinkest I am in sport; I pray thee tell me truly how thou likest her.

BENEDICK Would you buy her, that you inquire after her?

CLAUDIO Can the world buy such a jewel?

170 BENEDICK Yea, and a case to put it into. But speak you this with a sad brow? Or do you play the flouting Jack, to tell us Cupid is a good hare-finder, and Vulcan a rare carpenter? Come, in what key shall a man take you to go in the song?

CLAUDIO In mine eye she is the sweetest lady that ever I looked on.

BENEDICK I can see yet without spectacles, and I see no such matter; there's her cousin, an she were not possessed with a fury, exceeds her as much in beauty as the

180 first of May doth the last of December. But I hope you have no intent to turn husband, have you?

CLAUDIO I would scarce trust myself, though I had sworn the contrary, if Hero would be my wife.

BENEDICK Is't come to this? In faith, hath not the world one man but he will wear his cap with suspicion? Shall I never see a bachelor of threescore again? Go to, i'faith; an thou wilt needs thrust thy neck into a yoke, wear the print of it, and sigh away Sundays. Look, Don Pedro is returned to seek you.

Enter Don Pedro

DON PEDRO What secret hath held you here, that you   190
  followed not to Leonato's?

BENEDICK I would your grace would constrain me to tell.

DON PEDRO I charge thee on thy allegiance.

BENEDICK You hear, Count Claudio; I can be secret as a
  dumb man, I would have you think so; but, on my allegiance, mark you this, on my allegiance – he is in love.
  With who? Now that is your grace's part. Mark how short
  his answer is: With Hero, Leonato's short daughter.

CLAUDIO If this were so, so were it uttered.

BENEDICK Like the old tale, my lord: 'It is not so, nor   200
  'twas not so; but, indeed, God forbid it should be so!'

CLAUDIO If my passion change not shortly, God forbid it
  should be otherwise!

DON PEDRO Amen, if you love her; for the lady is very
  well worthy.

CLAUDIO You speak this to fetch me in, my lord.

DON PEDRO By my troth, I speak my thought.

CLAUDIO And in faith, my lord, I spoke mine.

BENEDICK And by my two faiths and troths, my lord, I
  spoke mine.   210

CLAUDIO That I love her, I feel.

DON PEDRO That she is worthy, I know.

BENEDICK That I neither feel how she should be loved,
  nor know how she should be worthy, is the opinion that
  fire cannot melt out of me; I will die in it at the stake.

DON PEDRO Thou wast ever an obstinate heretic in the
  despite of beauty.

CLAUDIO And never could maintain his part but in the
  force of his will.

BENEDICK That a woman conceived me, I thank her; that   220
  she brought me up, I likewise give her most humble
  thanks; but that I will have a recheat winded in my

forehead, or hang my bugle in an invisible baldrick, all
women shall pardon me. Because I will not do them the
wrong to mistrust any, I will do myself the right to trust
none; and the fine is, for the which I may go the finer, I
will live a bachelor.

DON PEDRO I shall see thee, ere I die, look pale with love.

BENEDICK With anger, with sickness, or with hunger, my
230   lord, not with love. Prove that ever I lose more blood
with love than I will get again with drinking, pick out
mine eyes with a ballad-maker's pen and hang me up
at the door of a brothel-house for the sign of blind
Cupid.

DON PEDRO Well, if ever thou dost fall from this faith,
thou wilt prove a notable argument.

BENEDICK If I do, hang me in a bottle like a cat, and shoot
at me; and he that hits me, let him be clapped on the
shoulder, and called Adam.

240 DON PEDRO Well, as time shall try:
    'In time the savage bull doth bear the yoke.'

BENEDICK The savage bull may; but if ever the sensible
Benedick bear it, pluck off the bull's horns and set them
in my forehead, and let me be vilely painted; and in such
great letters as they write 'Here is good horse to hire',
let them signify under my sign 'Here you may see
Benedick the married man.'

CLAUDIO If this should ever happen, thou wouldst be
horn-mad.

250 DON PEDRO Nay, if Cupid have not spent all his quiver in
Venice, thou wilt quake for this shortly.

BENEDICK I look for an earthquake too, then.

DON PEDRO Well, you will temporize with the hours. In
the meantime, good Signor Benedick, repair to Leonato's, commend me to him and tell him I will not fail
him at supper; for indeed he hath made great preparation.

BENEDICK I have almost matter enough in me for such an
    embassage; and so I commit you —

CLAUDIO To the tuition of God. From my house, if I had   260
    it —

DON PEDRO The sixth of July. Your loving friend,
    Benedick.

BENEDICK Nay, mock not, mock not. The body of your
    discourse is sometime guarded with fragments, and the
    guards are but slightly basted on neither. Ere you flout
    old ends any further, examine your conscience; and so I
    leave you.   *Exit*

CLAUDIO
    My liege, your highness now may do me good.

DON PEDRO
    My love is thine to teach; teach it but how,   270
    And thou shalt see how apt it is to learn
    Any hard lesson that may do thee good.

CLAUDIO
    Hath Leonato any son, my lord?

DON PEDRO
    No child but Hero; she's his only heir.
    Dost thou affect her, Claudio?

CLAUDIO   O, my lord,
    When you went onward on this ended action,
    I looked upon her with a soldier's eye,
    That liked, but had a rougher task in hand
    Than to drive liking to the name of love;
    But now I am returned and that war-thoughts   280
    Have left their places vacant, in their rooms
    Come thronging soft and delicate desires,
    All prompting me how fair young Hero is,
    Saying I liked her ere I went to wars.

DON PEDRO
    Thou wilt be like a lover presently

And tire the hearer with a book of words.
If thou dost love fair Hero, cherish it,
And I will break with her and with her father
And thou shalt have her. Was't not to this end
290   That thou began'st to twist so fine a story?

CLAUDIO
How sweetly you do minister to love,
That know love's grief by his complexion!
But lest my liking might too sudden seem,
I would have salved it with a longer treatise.

DON PEDRO
What need the bridge much broader than the flood?
The fairest grant is the necessity.
Look what will serve is fit. 'Tis once, thou lovest,
And I will fit thee with the remedy.
I know we shall have revelling tonight;
300   I will assume thy part in some disguise
And tell fair Hero I am Claudio,
And in her bosom I'll unclasp my heart,
And take her hearing prisoner with the force
And strong encounter of my amorous tale.
Then after, to her father will I break,
And the conclusion is, she shall be thine.
In practice let us put it presently.   *Exeunt*

I.2   *Enter Leonato meeting an old man, his brother Antonio*
LEONATO How now, brother! Where is my cousin, your
    son? Hath he provided this music?
ANTONIO He is very busy about it. But, brother, I can tell
    you strange news that you yet dreamt not of.
LEONATO Are they good?
ANTONIO As the event stamps them; but they have a
    good cover, they show well outward. The Prince and

Count Claudio, walking in a thick-pleached alley in
mine orchard, were thus much overheard by a man of
mine: the Prince discovered to Claudio that he loved   10
my niece your daughter, and meant to acknowledge it
this night in a dance; and if he found her accordant, he
meant to take the present time by the top and instantly
break with you of it.

LEONATO Hath the fellow any wit that told you this?

ANTONIO A good sharp fellow; I will send for him, and
question him yourself.

LEONATO No, no; we will hold it as a dream, till it appear
itself; but I will acquaint my daughter withal, that she
be the better prepared for an answer, if peradventure   20
this be true. Go you and tell her of it.

Attendants cross the stage, led by Antonio's son, and
accompanied by Balthasar the musician

Cousin, you know what you have to do. (*To the musician*)
O, I cry you mercy, friend; go you with me, and I will
use your skill. Good cousin, have a care this busy time.

Exeunt

Enter Don John the Bastard and Conrade his   I.3
companion

CONRADE What the good-year, my lord! Why are you thus
out of measure sad?

DON JOHN There is no measure in the occasion that
breeds; therefore the sadness is without limit.

CONRADE You should hear reason.

DON JOHN And when I have heard it, what blessing brings
it?

CONRADE If not a present remedy, at least a patient
sufferance.

DON JOHN I wonder that thou—being, as thou sayest thou   10

art, born under Saturn — goest about to apply a moral
medicine to a mortifying mischief. I cannot hide what
I am. I must be sad when I have cause, and smile at no
man's jests; eat when I have stomach, and wait for no
man's leisure; sleep when I am drowsy, and tend on no
man's business; laugh when I am merry, and claw no
man in his humour.

CONRADE Yea, but you must not make the full show of this
till you may do it without controlment. You have of late
stood out against your brother, and he hath ta'en you
newly into his grace, where it is impossible you should
take true root but by the fair weather that you make
yourself; it is needful that you frame the season for your
own harvest.

DON JOHN I had rather be a canker in a hedge than a rose
in his grace, and it better fits my blood to be disdained
of all than to fashion a carriage to rob love from any. In
this, though I cannot be said to be a flattering honest
man, it must not be denied but I am a plain-dealing
villain. I am trusted with a muzzle and enfranchised with
a clog; therefore I have decreed not to sing in my cage.
If I had my mouth, I would bite; if I had my liberty, I
would do my liking. In the meantime, let me be that I
am, and seek not to alter me.

CONRADE Can you make no use of your discontent?

DON JOHN I make all use of it, for I use it only. Who
comes here?

Enter Borachio

What news, Borachio?

BORACHIO I came yonder from a great supper. The Prince
your brother is royally entertained by Leonato; and I can
give you intelligence of an intended marriage.

DON JOHN Will it serve for any model to build mischief
on? What is he for a fool that betroths himself to
unquietness?

BORACHIO Marry, it is your brother's right hand.

DON JOHN Who? The most exquisite Claudio?

BORACHIO Even he.

DON JOHN A proper squire! And who, and who? Which way looks he?

BORACHIO Marry, on Hero, the daughter and heir of 50
Leonato.

DON JOHN A very forward March-chick! How came you to this?

BORACHIO Being entertained for a perfumer, as I was smoking a musty room, comes me the Prince and Claudio, hand in hand, in sad conference. I whipt me behind the arras, and there heard it agreed upon that the Prince should woo Hero for himself, and having obtained her, give her to Count Claudio.

DON JOHN Come, come, let us thither; this may prove 60
food to my displeasure. That young start-up hath all the glory of my overthrow; if I can cross him any way, I bless myself every way. You are both sure, and will assist me?

CONRADE To the death, my lord.

DON JOHN Let us to the great supper; their cheer is the greater that I am subdued. Would the cook were o'my mind! Shall we go prove what's to be done?

BORACHIO We'll wait upon your lordship.   *Exeunt*

*

Enter Leonato, Antonio, Hero, Beatrice, Margaret,   II.1
and Ursula

LEONATO Was not Count John here at supper?

ANTONIO I saw him not.

BEATRICE How tartly that gentleman looks! I never can see

him but I am heart-burned an hour after.

HERO He is of a very melancholy disposition.

BEATRICE He were an excellent man that were made just
in the midway between him and Benedick; the one is
too like an image and says nothing, and the other too
like my lady's eldest son, evermore tattling.

10 LEONATO Then half Signor Benedick's tongue in Count
John's mouth, and half Count John's melancholy in
Signor Benedick's face –

BEATRICE With a good leg and a good foot, uncle, and
money enough in his purse, such a man would win any
woman in the world, if 'a could get her good will.

LEONATO By my troth, niece, thou wilt never get thee a
husband if thou be so shrewd of thy tongue.

ANTONIO In faith, she's too curst.

BEATRICE Too curst is more than curst. I shall lessen
20 God's sending that way; for it is said, 'God sends a curst
cow short horns', but to a cow too curst he sends none.

LEONATO So, by being too curst, God will send you no
horns.

BEATRICE Just, if he send me no husband; for the which
blessing I am at him upon my knees every morning and
evening. Lord, I could not endure a husband with a
beard on his face! I had rather lie in the woollen.

LEONATO You may light on a husband that hath no beard.

BEATRICE What should I do with him? Dress him in my
30 apparel and make him my waiting-gentlewoman? He
that hath a beard is more than a youth, and he that hath
no beard is less than a man; and he that is more than a
youth is not for me, and he that is less than a man, I am
not for him. Therefore I will even take sixpence in
earnest of the bear-ward, and lead his apes into hell.

LEONATO Well then, go you into hell?

BEATRICE No, but to the gate; and there will the devil

meet me, like an old cuckold with horns on his head,
and say 'Get you to heaven, Beatrice, get you to heaven;
here's no place for you maids.' So deliver I up my apes,   40
and away to Saint Peter for the heavens; he shows me
where the bachelors sit, and there live we as merry as
the day is long.

ANTONIO (*to Hero*) Well, niece, I trust you will be ruled
     by your father.

BEATRICE Yes, faith; it is my cousin's duty to make
     curtsy and say, 'Father, as it please you.' But yet for all
     that, cousin, let him be a handsome fellow, or else make
     another curtsy and say, 'Father, as it please me.'

LEONATO Well, niece, I hope to see you one day fitted with   50
     a husband.

BEATRICE Not till God make men of some other metal
     than earth. Would it not grieve a woman to be over-
     mastered with a piece of valiant dust? To make an
     account of her life to a clod of wayward marl? No,
     uncle, I'll none. Adam's sons are my brethren, and,
     truly, I hold it a sin to match in my kindred.

LEONATO Daughter, remember what I told you. If the
     Prince do solicit you in that kind, you know your
     answer.   60

BEATRICE The fault will be in the music, cousin, if you
     be not wooed in good time. If the Prince be too impor-
     tant, tell him there is measure in everything and so dance
     out the answer. For hear me, Hero: wooing, wedding,
     and repenting, is as a Scotch jig, a measure, and a
     cinquepace; the first suit is hot and hasty, like a Scotch
     jig, and full as fantastical; the wedding, mannerly-
     modest, as a measure, full of state and ancientry; and
     then comes repentance and, with his bad legs, falls into
     the cinquepace faster and faster, till he sink into his   70
     grave.

LEONATO Cousin, you apprehend passing shrewdly.

BEATRICE I have a good eye, uncle; I can see a church by daylight.

LEONATO The revellers are entering, brother; make good room.

> *All put on their masks*
> *Enter Don Pedro, Claudio, Benedick, Balthasar, Don John, Borachio and others, as masquers, with a drum*

DON PEDRO Lady, will you walk a bout with your friend?

HERO So you walk softly, and look sweetly, and say nothing, I am yours for the walk; and especially when
80   I walk away.

DON PEDRO With me in your company?

HERO I may say so, when I please.

DON PEDRO And when please you to say so?

HERO When I like your favour; for God defend the lute should be like the case!

DON PEDRO
> My visor is Philemon's roof; within the house is Jove.

HERO
> Why, then, your visor should be thatched.

DON PEDRO   Speak low, if you speak love.

> *He draws her aside*

BALTHASAR Well, I would you did like me.

MARGARET So would not I, for your own sake; for I have
90   many ill qualities.

BALTHASAR Which is one?

MARGARET I say my prayers aloud.

BALTHASAR I love you the better; the hearers may cry Amen.

MARGARET God match me with a good dancer!

BALTHASAR Amen.

MARGARET And God keep him out of my sight when the dance is done! Answer, clerk.

BALTHASAR No more words; the clerk is answered.

URSULA I know you well enough; you are Signor Antonio.   100

ANTONIO At a word, I am not.

URSULA I know you by the waggling of your head.

ANTONIO To tell you true, I counterfeit him.

URSULA You could never do him so ill-well unless you
    were the very man. Here's his dry hand up and down;
    you are he, you are he.

ANTONIO At a word, I am not.

URSULA Come, come, do you think I do not know you by
    your excellent wit? Can virtue hide itself? Go to, mum,
    you are he; graces will appear, and there's an end.   110

BEATRICE Will you not tell me who told you so?

BENEDICK No, you shall pardon me.

BEATRICE Nor will you not tell me who you are?

BENEDICK Not now.

BEATRICE That I was disdainful, and that I had my good
    wit out of the 'Hundred Merry Tales' – well, this was
    Signor Benedick that said so.

BENEDICK What's he?

BEATRICE I am sure you know him well enough.

BENEDICK Not I, believe me.   120

BEATRICE Did he never make you laugh?

BENEDICK I pray you, what is he?

BEATRICE Why, he is the Prince's jester, a very dull fool;
    only his gift is in devising impossible slanders. None but
    libertines delight in him, and the commendation is not
    in his wit, but in his villainy; for he both pleases men
    and angers them, and then they laugh at him and beat
    him. I am sure he is in the fleet; I would he had boarded
    me.

BENEDICK When I know the gentleman, I'll tell him what   130
    you say.

BEATRICE Do, do; he'll but break a comparison or two

on me, which, peradventure not marked or not laughed at, strikes him into melancholy; and then there's a partridge wing saved, for the fool will eat no supper that night.

Music for the dance

We must follow the leaders.

BENEDICK In every good thing.

BEATRICE Nay, if they lead to any ill, I will leave them at
140   the next turning.

Exeunt all dancing, except Don John,
Borachio, and Claudio

DON JOHN Sure my brother is amorous on Hero and hath withdrawn her father to break with him about it. The ladies follow her and but one visor remains.

BORACHIO And that is Claudio; I know him by his bearing.

DON JOHN Are not you Signor Benedick?

CLAUDIO You know me well; I am he.

DON JOHN Signor, you are very near my brother in his love. He is enamoured on Hero; I pray you dissuade
150   him from her; she is no equal for his birth. You may do the part of an honest man in it.

CLAUDIO How know you he loves her?

DON JOHN I heard him swear his affection.

BORACHIO So did I too, and he swore he would marry her tonight.

DON JOHN Come, let us to the banquet.

Exeunt Don John and Borachio

CLAUDIO

Thus answer I in name of Benedick,

But hear these ill news with the ears of Claudio.

'Tis certain so; the Prince woos for himself.
160   Friendship is constant in all other things

Save in the office and affairs of love;

Therefore all hearts in love use their own tongues.
Let every eye negotiate for itself,
And trust no agent; for beauty is a witch
Against whose charms faith melteth into blood.
This is an accident of hourly proof,
Which I mistrusted not. Farewell therefore, Hero!

Enter Benedick

BENEDICK Count Claudio?

CLAUDIO Yea, the same.

BENEDICK Come, will you go with me?   170

CLAUDIO Whither?

BENEDICK Even to the next willow, about your own business, County. What fashion will you wear the garland
of? About your neck, like an usurer's chain? Or under
your arm, like a lieutenant's scarf? You must wear it
one way, for the Prince hath got your Hero.

CLAUDIO I wish him joy of her.

BENEDICK Why, that's spoken like an honest drovier; so
they sell bullocks. But did you think the Prince would
have served you thus?   180

CLAUDIO I pray you, leave me.

BENEDICK Ho! Now you strike like the blind man; 'twas
the boy that stole your meat, and you'll beat the post.

CLAUDIO If it will not be, I'll leave you.   *Exit*

BENEDICK Alas, poor hurt fowl, now will he creep into
sedges! But that my Lady Beatrice should know me,
and not know me! The Prince's fool! Ha? It may be I
go under that title because I am merry. Yea, but so I am
apt to do myself wrong. I am not so reputed; it is the
base, though bitter, disposition of Beatrice that puts the   190
world into her person, and so gives me out. Well, I'll be
revenged as I may.

Enter Don Pedro, with Leonato and Hero

DON PEDRO Now, signor, where's the Count? Did you
see him?

BENEDICK Troth, my lord, I have played the part of Lady
Fame. I found him here as melancholy as a lodge in a
warren; I told him, and I think I told him true, that
your grace had got the good will of this young lady; and
I offered him my company to a willow-tree, either to
make him a garland, as being forsaken, or to bind him
up a rod, as being worthy to be whipped.

DON PEDRO To be whipped! What's his fault?

BENEDICK The flat transgression of a schoolboy, who,
being overjoyed with finding a bird's nest, shows it his
companion, and he steals it.

DON PEDRO Wilt thou make a trust a transgression? The
transgression is in the stealer.

BENEDICK Yet it had not been amiss the rod had been
made, and the garland too; for the garland he might
have worn himself, and the rod he might have bestowed
on you, who, as I take it, have stolen his bird's nest.

DON PEDRO I will but teach them to sing, and restore them
to the owner.

BENEDICK If their singing answer your saying, by my
faith you say honestly.

DON PEDRO The Lady Beatrice hath a quarrel to you; the
gentleman that danced with her told her she is much
wronged by you.

BENEDICK O, she misused me past the endurance of a
block! An oak but with one green leaf on it would have
answered her; my very visor began to assume life and
scold with her. She told me, not thinking I had been
myself, that I was the Prince's jester, that I was duller
than a great thaw; huddling jest upon jest with such
impossible conveyance upon me that I stood like a man
at a mark, with a whole army shooting at me. She
speaks poniards, and every word stabs. If her breath
were as terrible as her terminations, there were no living

near her; she would infect to the north star. I would not
marry her, though she were endowed with all that   230
Adam had left him before he transgressed. She would
have made Hercules have turned spit, yea, and have cleft
his club to make the fire too. Come, talk not of her; you
shall find her the infernal Ate in good apparel. I would to
God some scholar would conjure her; for certainly, while
she is here, a man may live as quiet in hell as in a sanctuary, and people sin upon purpose, because they would
go thither; so, indeed, all disquiet, horror, and pertur-
bation follows her.

    Enter Claudio and Beatrice

DON PEDRO Look, here she comes.   240

BENEDICK Will your grace command me any service to
    the world's end? I will go on the slightest errand now
    to the Antipodes that you can devise to send me on. I
    will fetch you a tooth-picker now from the furthest inch
    of Asia; bring you the length of Prester John's foot;
    fetch you a hair off the great Cham's beard; do you any
    embassage to the Pigmies, rather than hold three words'
    conference with this harpy. You have no employment
    for me?

DON PEDRO None, but to desire your good company.   250

BENEDICK O God, sir, here's a dish I love not; I cannot
    endure my Lady Tongue.   *Exit*

DON PEDRO Come, lady, come; you have lost the heart of
    Signor Benedick.

BEATRICE Indeed, my lord, he lent it me awhile, and I
    gave him use for it, a double heart for his single one.
    Marry, once before he won it of me with false dice,
    therefore your grace may well say I have lost it.

DON PEDRO You have put him down, lady, you have put
    him down.   260

BEATRICE So I would not he should do me, my lord, lest

I should prove the mother of fools. I have brought
Count Claudio, whom you sent me to seek.

DON PEDRO Why, how now, Count! Wherefore are you
sad?

CLAUDIO Not sad, my lord.

DON PEDRO How then? Sick?

CLAUDIO Neither, my lord.

BEATRICE The Count is neither sad, nor sick, nor merry,
270   nor well; but civil count, civil as an orange, and something of that jealous complexion.

DON PEDRO I'faith, lady, I think your blazon to be true,
though, I'll be sworn, if he be so, his conceit is false.
Here, Claudio, I have wooed in thy name, and fair
Hero is won. I have broke with her father, and his
will obtained; name the day of marriage, and God give
thee joy!

LEONATO Count, take of me my daughter, and with her
my fortunes. His grace hath made the match, and all
280   Grace say Amen to it!

BEATRICE Speak, Count, 'tis your cue.

CLAUDIO Silence is the perfectest herald of joy; I were
but little happy, if I could say how much. Lady, as you
are mine, I am yours; I give away myself for you and
dote upon the exchange.

BEATRICE Speak, cousin; or, if you cannot, stop his mouth
with a kiss, and let not him speak neither.

DON PEDRO In faith, lady, you have a merry heart.

BEATRICE Yea, my lord; I thank it, poor fool, it keeps on
290   the windy side of care. My cousin tells him in his ear
that he is in her heart.

CLAUDIO And so she doth, cousin.

BEATRICE Good Lord, for alliance! Thus goes every one
to the world but I, and I am sunburnt; I may sit in a
corner and cry 'Heigh-ho for a husband!'

DON PEDRO Lady Beatrice, I will get you one.

BEATRICE I would rather have one of your father's getting. Hath your grace ne'er a brother like you? Your
father got excellent husbands, if a maid could come by
them.   300

DON PEDRO Will you have me, lady?

BEATRICE No, my lord, unless I might have another for
working-days: your grace is too costly to wear every
day. But, I beseech your grace, pardon me; I was born
to speak all mirth and no matter.

DON PEDRO Your silence most offends me, and to be
merry best becomes you; for, out o'question, you were
born in a merry hour.

BEATRICE No, sure, my lord, my mother cried; but then
there was a star danced, and under that was I born.   310
Cousins, God give you joy!

LEONATO Niece, will you look to those things I told you
of?

BEATRICE I cry you mercy, uncle. (*To Don Pedro*) By
your grace's pardon.   *Exit*

DON PEDRO By my troth, a pleasant-spirited lady.

LEONATO There's little of the melancholy element in her,
my lord; she is never sad but when she sleeps, and not
ever sad then; for I have heard my daughter say, she hath
often dreamt of unhappiness and waked herself with   320
laughing.

DON PEDRO She cannot endure to hear tell of a husband.

LEONATO O, by no means; she mocks all her wooers out
of suit.

DON PEDRO She were an excellent wife for Benedick.

LEONATO O Lord, my lord, if they were but a week
married, they would talk themselves mad.

DON PEDRO County Claudio, when mean you to go to
church?

330 CLAUDIO Tomorrow, my lord. Time goes on crutches
till love have all his rites.

LEONATO Not till Monday, my dear son, which is hence
a just seven-night; and a time too brief, too, to have all
things answer my mind.

DON PEDRO Come, you shake the head at so long a
breathing; but, I warrant thee, Claudio, the time shall
not go dully by us. I will in the interim undertake one
of Hercules' labours; which is, to bring Signor Benedick
and the Lady Beatrice into a mountain of affection,
340 th'one with th'other. I would fain have it a match, and
I doubt not but to fashion it, if you three will but
minister such assistance as I shall give you direction.

LEONATO My lord, I am for you, though it cost me ten
nights' watchings.

CLAUDIO And I, my lord.

DON PEDRO And you too, gentle Hero?

HERO I will do any modest office, my lord, to help my
cousin to a good husband.

DON PEDRO And Benedick is not the unhopefullest hus-
350 band that I know. Thus far can I praise him: he is of a
noble strain, of approved valour and confirmed honesty.
I will teach you how to humour your cousin, that she
shall fall in love with Benedick; and I, with your two
helps, will so practise on Benedick that, in despite of
his quick wit and his queasy stomach, he shall fall in
love with Beatrice. If we can do this, Cupid is no
longer an archer; his glory shall be ours, for we are the
only love-gods. Go in with me, and I will tell you my
drift.   *Exeunt*

Enter Don John and Borachio   II.2

DON JOHN It is so; the Count Claudio shall marry the
  daughter of Leonato.

BORACHIO Yea, my lord, but I can cross it.

DON JOHN Any bar, any cross, any impediment will be
  medicinable to me: I am sick in displeasure to him,
  and whatsoever comes athwart his affection ranges
  evenly with mine. How canst thou cross this marriage?

BORACHIO Not honestly, my lord; but so covertly that
  no dishonesty shall appear in me.

DON JOHN Show me briefly how.   10

BORACHIO I think I told your lordship a year since, how
  much I am in the favour of Margaret, the waiting-
  gentlewoman to Hero.

DON JOHN I remember.

BORACHIO I can, at any unseasonable instant of the night,
  appoint her to look out at her lady's chamber-window.

DON JOHN What life is in that, to be the death of this
  marriage?

BORACHIO The poison of that lies in you to temper. Go
  you to the Prince your brother; spare not to tell him   20
  that he hath wronged his honour in marrying the re-
  nowned Claudio — whose estimation do you mightily
  hold up — to a contaminated stale, such a one as Hero.

DON JOHN What proof shall I make of that?

BORACHIO Proof enough to misuse the Prince, to vex
  Claudio, to undo Hero and kill Leonato. Look you for
  any other issue?

DON JOHN Only to despite them I will endeavour anything.

BORACHIO Go, then; find me a meet hour to draw Don   30
  Pedro and the Count Claudio alone. Tell them that
  you know that Hero loves me; intend a kind of zeal both
  to the Prince and Claudio — as in love of your brother's

honour, who hath made this match, and his friend's
reputation, who is thus like to be cozened with the semblance of a maid – that you have discovered thus. They
will scarcely believe this without trial; offer them
instances, which shall bear no less likelihood than to
see me at her chamber window, hear me call Margaret
40   Hero, hear Margaret term me Claudio; and bring them
to see this the very night before the intended wedding –
for in the meantime I will so fashion the matter that
Hero shall be absent – and there shall appear such seeming truth of Hero's disloyalty that jealousy shall be called
assurance, and all the preparation overthrown.

DON JOHN Grow this to what adverse issue it can, I will
put it in practice. Be cunning in the working this, and
thy fee is a thousand ducats.

BORACHIO Be you constant in the accusation, and my
50   cunning shall not shame me.

DON JOHN I will presently go learn their day of marriage.
                                              Exeunt

II.3   *Enter Benedick alone*
BENEDICK Boy!
           Enter Boy
BOY Signor?
BENEDICK In my chamber-window lies a book; bring it
    hither to me in the orchard.
BOY I am here already, sir.
BENEDICK I know that; but I would have thee hence, and
    here again.   *Exit Boy*
    I do much wonder that one man, seeing how much
    another man is a fool when he dedicates his behaviours
10   to love, will, after he hath laughed at such shallow
    follies in others, become the argument of his own

scorn by falling in love; and such a man is Claudio. I
have known when there was no music with him but the
drum and the fife, and now had he rather hear the tabor
and the pipe. I have known when he would have walked
ten mile afoot to see a good armour, and now will he lie
ten nights awake carving the fashion of a new doublet.
He was wont to speak plain and to the purpose, like an
honest man and a soldier, and now is he turned orthography; his words are a very fantastical banquet, just so   20
many strange dishes. May I be so converted and see with
these eyes? I cannot tell; I think not. I will not be
sworn but love may transform me to an oyster; but I'll
take my oath on it, till he have made an oyster of me, he
shall never make me such a fool. One woman is fair, yet
I am well; another is wise, yet I am well; another virtuous, yet I am well; but till all graces be in one woman,
one woman shall not come in my grace. Rich she shall
be, that's certain; wise, or I'll none; virtuous, or I'll
never cheapen her; fair, or I'll never look on her; mild,   30
or come not near me; noble, or not I for an angel; of
good discourse, an excellent musician, and her hair shall
be of what colour it please God. Ha! The Prince and
Monsieur Love! I will hide me in the arbour.

He withdraws

Enter Don Pedro, Leonato, and Claudio

DON PEDRO

Come, shall we hear this music?

CLAUDIO

Yea, my good lord. How still the evening is,
As hushed on purpose to grace harmony!

DON PEDRO

See you where Benedick hath hid himself?

CLAUDIO

O, very well, my lord; the music ended,

40   We'll fit the hid-fox with a pennyworth.
        Enter Balthasar with music

DON PEDRO
    Come, Balthasar, we'll hear that song again.

BALTHASAR
    O, good my lord, tax not so bad a voice
    To slander music any more than once.

DON PEDRO
    It is the witness still of excellency
    To put a strange face on his own perfection.
    I pray thee sing, and let me woo no more.

BALTHASAR
    Because you talk of wooing, I will sing,
    Since many a wooer doth commence his suit
    To her he thinks not worthy; yet he woos,
50   Yet will he swear he loves.

DON PEDRO   Nay, pray thee, come;
    Or, if thou wilt hold longer argument,
    Do it in notes.

BALTHASAR   Note this before my notes;
    There's not a note of mine that's worth the noting.

DON PEDRO
    Why, these are very crotchets that he speaks;
    Note notes, forsooth, and nothing.
        Music

BENEDICK Now, divine air! Now is his soul ravished! Is
    it not strange that sheep's guts should hale souls out of
    men's bodies? Well, a horn for my money, when all's
    done.

BALTHASAR   *The Song*

60   Sigh no more, ladies, sigh no more,
                Men were deceivers ever,
            One foot in sea and one on shore,
                To one thing constant never:

    Then sigh not so, but let them go,
      And be you blithe and bonny,
    Converting all your sounds of woe
      Into Hey nonny, nonny.

    Sing no more ditties, sing no moe,
      Of dumps so dull and heavy;
    The fraud of men was ever so,   70
      Since summer first was leavy:
    Then sigh not so, but let them go,
      And be you blithe and bonny,
    Converting all your sounds of woe
      Into Hey nonny, nonny.

DON PEDRO By my troth, a good song.

BALTHASAR And an ill singer, my lord.

DON PEDRO Ha, no, no, faith; thou singest well enough for a shift.

BENEDICK An he had been a dog that should have   80 howled thus, they would have hanged him; and I pray God his bad voice bode no mischief. I had as lief have heard the night-raven, come what plague could have come after it.

DON PEDRO Yea, marry, dost thou hear, Balthasar? I pray thee, get us some excellent music; for tomorrow night we would have it at the Lady Hero's chamber-window.

BALTHASAR The best I can, my lord.

DON PEDRO Do so; farewell.   *Exit Balthasar* 90
Come hither, Leonato. What was it you told me of to-day, that your niece Beatrice was in love with Signor Benedick?

CLAUDIO (*aside*) O, ay; stalk on, stalk on, the fowl sits. – I did never think that lady would have loved any man.

LEONATO No, nor I neither; but most wonderful that
she should dote so on Signor Benedick, whom she hath
in all outward behaviours seemed ever to abhor.

BENEDICK (*aside*) Is't possible? Sits the wind in that
corner?

LEONATO By my troth, my lord, I cannot tell what to
think of it; but that she loves him with an enraged affection, it is past the infinite of thought.

DON PEDRO May be she doth but counterfeit.

CLAUDIO Faith, like enough.

LEONATO O God! Counterfeit? There was never counterfeit of passion came so near the life of passion as she
discovers it.

DON PEDRO Why, what effects of passion shows she?

CLAUDIO (*to Don Pedro and Leonato*) Bait the hook well;
this fish will bite.

LEONATO What effects, my lord? She will sit you – you
heard my daughter tell you how.

CLAUDIO She did, indeed.

DON PEDRO How, how, I pray you? You amaze me; I
would have thought her spirit had been invincible
against all assaults of affection.

LEONATO I would have sworn it had, my lord, especially
against Benedick.

BENEDICK (*aside*) I should think this a gull, but that the
white-bearded fellow speaks it; knavery cannot, sure,
hide himself in such reverence.

CLAUDIO (*to Don Pedro and Leonato*) He hath ta'en the
infection; hold it up.

DON PEDRO Hath she made her affection known to
Benedick?

LEONATO No, and swears she never will; that's her
torment.

CLAUDIO 'Tis true, indeed, so your daughter says. 'Shall

I,' says she, 'that have so oft encountered him with   130
scorn, write to him that I love him?'

LEONATO This says she now when she is beginning to
write to him; for she'll be up twenty times a night, and
there will she sit in her smock till she have writ a sheet
of paper. My daughter tells us all.

CLAUDIO Now you talk of a sheet of paper, I remember
a pretty jest your daughter told us of.

LEONATO O, when she had writ it and was reading it
over, she found Benedick and Beatrice between the
sheet?   140

CLAUDIO That.

LEONATO O, she tore the letter into a thousand halfpence; railed at herself, that she should be so immodest to write to one that she knew would flout her.
'I measure him,' says she, 'by my own spirit; for I
should flout him, if he writ to me; yea, though I love
him, I should.'

CLAUDIO Then down upon her knees she falls, weeps,
sobs, beats her heart, tears her hair, prays, curses – 'O
sweet Benedick! God give me patience!'   150

LEONATO She doth indeed, my daughter says so; and the
ecstasy hath so much overborne her that my daughter
is sometime afeard she will do a desperate outrage to
herself. It is very true.

DON PEDRO It were good that Benedick knew of it by
some other, if she will not discover it.

CLAUDIO To what end? He would make but a sport of it
and torment the poor lady worse.

DON PEDRO An he should, it were an alms to hang him.
She's an excellent sweet lady, and, out of all suspicion, 160
she is virtuous.

CLAUDIO And she is exceeding wise.

DON PEDRO In every thing but in loving Benedick.

LEONATO O, my lord, wisdom and blood combating in so
tender a body, we have ten proofs to one that blood
hath the victory. I am sorry for her, as I have just cause,
being her uncle and her guardian.

DON PEDRO I would she had bestowed this dotage on me;
I would have daffed all other respects and made her half
170   myself. I pray you, tell Benedick of it, and hear what
'a will say.

LEONATO Were it good, think you?

CLAUDIO Hero thinks surely she will die; for she says she
will die, if he love her not; and she will die, ere she make
her love known; and she will die if he woo her, rather
than she will bate one breath of her accustomed cross-
ness.

DON PEDRO She doth well. If she should make tender of
her love, 'tis very possible he'll scorn it; for the man,
180   as you know all, hath a contemptible spirit.

CLAUDIO He is a very proper man.

DON PEDRO He hath, indeed, a good outward happiness.

CLAUDIO Before God, and in my mind, very wise.

DON PEDRO He doth, indeed, show some sparks that are
like wit.

CLAUDIO And I take him to be valiant.

DON PEDRO As Hector, I assure you; and in the man-
aging of quarrels you may say he is wise, for either he
avoids them with great discretion, or undertakes them
190   with a most Christian-like fear.

LEONATO If he do fear God, 'a must necessarily keep
peace; if he break the peace, he ought to enter into a
quarrel with fear and trembling.

DON PEDRO And so will he do, for the man doth fear God,
howsoever it seems not in him by some large jests he
will make. Well, I am sorry for your niece. Shall we go
seek Benedick, and tell him of her love?

CLAUDIO Never tell him, my lord; let her wear it out with
    good counsel.

LEONATO Nay, that's impossible; she may wear her heart   200
    out first.

DON PEDRO Well, we will hear further of it by your
    daughter; let it cool the while. I love Benedick well; and
    I could wish he would modestly examine himself, to see
    how much he is unworthy so good a lady.

LEONATO My lord, will you walk? Dinner is ready.

CLAUDIO (*aside*) If he do not dote on her upon this, I will
    never trust my expectation.

DON PEDRO (*to Leonato*) Let there be the same net spread
    for her, and that must your daughter and her gentle-   210
    women carry. The sport will be, when they hold one
    an opinion of another's dotage, and no such matter;
    that's the scene that I would see, which will be merely a
    dumb-show. Let us send her to call him in to dinner.

               Exeunt Don Pedro, Claudio, and Leonato

BENEDICK (*coming forward*) This can be no trick. The
    conference was sadly borne. They have the truth of this
    from Hero. They seem to pity the lady; it seems her
    affections have their full bent. Love me? Why, it must
    be requited. I heard how I am censured: they say I will
    bear myself proudly, if I perceive the love come from   220
    her; they say, too, that she will rather die than give any
    sign of affection. I did never think to marry. I must not
    seem proud; happy are they that hear their detractions
    and can put them to mending. They say the lady is fair;
    'tis a truth, I can bear them witness; and virtuous; so,
    I cannot reprove it; and wise, but for loving me. By my
    troth, it is no addition to her wit, nor no great argument
    of her folly, for I will be horribly in love with her. I may
    chance have some odd quirks and remnants of wit broken
    on me, because I have railed so long against marriage;   230

but doth not the appetite alter? A man loves the meat in his youth that he cannot endure in his age. Shall quips and sentences and these paper bullets of the brain awe a man from the career of his humour? No, the world must be peopled. When I said I would die a bachelor, I did not think I should live till I were married. Here comes Beatrice. By this day, she's a fair lady! I do spy some marks of love in her.

Enter Beatrice

BEATRICE Against my will I am sent to bid you come in to
240   dinner.

BENEDICK
    Fair Beatrice, I thank you for your pains.

BEATRICE I took no more pains for those thanks than you take pains to thank me; if it had been painful, I would not have come.

BENEDICK You take pleasure then in the message?

BEATRICE Yea, just so much as you may take upon a knife's point, and choke a daw withal. You have no stomach, signor; fare you well.   *Exit*

BENEDICK Ha! 'Against my will I am sent to bid you
250   come in to dinner' – there's a double meaning in that. 'I took no more pains for those thanks than you took pains to thank me' – that's as much as to say, 'Any pains that I take for you is as easy as thanks.' If I do not take pity of her, I am a villain; if I do not love her, I am a Jew. I will go get her picture.   *Exit*

*

III.1   *Enter Hero and two gentlewomen (Margaret and Ursula)*

HERO
    Good Margaret, run thee to the parlour;

There shalt thou find my cousin Beatrice
Proposing with the Prince and Claudio.
Whisper her ear, and tell her I and Ursula
Walk in the orchard, and our whole discourse
Is all of her; say that thou overheardst us,
And bid her steal into the pleachèd bower,
Where honeysuckles, ripened by the sun,
Forbid the sun to enter – like favourites,
Made proud by princes, that advance their pride   10
Against that power that bred it. There will she hide her,
To listen our propose. This is thy office;
Bear thee well in it, and leave us alone.

MARGARET
I'll make her come, I warrant you, presently.   *Exit*

HERO
Now, Ursula, when Beatrice doth come,
As we do trace this alley up and down,
Our talk must only be of Benedick;
When I do name him, let it be thy part
To praise him more than ever man did merit.
My talk to thee must be how Benedick   20
Is sick in love with Beatrice. Of this matter
Is little Cupid's crafty arrow made,
That only wounds by hearsay. Now begin;
     Enter Beatrice secretively. She slips into the bower
For look where Beatrice, like a lapwing, runs
Close by the ground, to hear our conference.

URSULA (*to Hero*)
The pleasant'st angling is to see the fish
Cut with her golden oars the silver stream,
And greedily devour the treacherous bait;
So angle we for Beatrice, who even now
Is couchèd in the woodbine coverture.   30
Fear you not my part of the dialogue.

HERO *(to Ursula)*

    Then go we near her, that her ear lose nothing
    Of the false sweet bait that we lay for it.

      They approach the bower

    No, truly, Ursula, she is too disdainful;
    I know her spirits are as coy and wild
    As haggards of the rock.

URSULA   But are you sure

    That Benedick loves Beatrice so entirely?

HERO

    So says the Prince and my new-trothèd lord.

URSULA

    And did they bid you tell her of it, madam?

HERO

40   They did entreat me to acquaint her of it;
    But I persuaded them, if they loved Benedick,
    To wish him wrestle with affection,
    And never to let Beatrice know of it.

URSULA

    Why did you so? Doth not the gentleman
    Deserve as full as fortunate a bed
    As ever Beatrice shall couch upon?

HERO

    O god of love! I know he doth deserve
    As much as may be yielded to a man;
    But Nature never framed a woman's heart
50   Of prouder stuff than that of Beatrice.
    Disdain and scorn ride sparkling in her eyes,
    Misprizing what they look on, and her wit
    Values itself so highly that to her
    All matter else seems weak. She cannot love,
    Nor take no shape nor project of affection,
    She is so self-endeared.

URSULA   Sure, I think so;

And therefore, certainly, it were not good
She knew his love, lest she'll make sport at it.

HERO

Why, you speak truth. I never yet saw man,
How wise, how noble, young, how rarely featured,   60
But she would spell him backward. If fair-faced,
She would swear the gentleman should be her sister;
If black, why, Nature, drawing of an antic,
Made a foul blot; if tall, a lance ill-headed;
If low, an agate very vilely cut;
If speaking, why, a vane blown with all winds;
If silent, why, a block movèd with none.
So turns she every man the wrong side out,
And never gives to truth and virtue that
Which simpleness and merit purchaseth.   70

URSULA

Sure, sure, such carping is not commendable.

HERO

No, not to be so odd and from all fashions
As Beatrice is, cannot be commendable;
But who dare tell her so? If I should speak,
She would mock me into air; O, she would laugh me
Out of myself, press me to death with wit!
Therefore let Benedick, like covered fire,
Consume away in sighs, waste inwardly.
It were a better death than die with mocks,
Which is as bad as die with tickling.   80

URSULA

Yet tell her of it; hear what she will say.

HERO

No; rather I will go to Benedick
And counsel him to fight against his passion.
And, truly, I'll devise some honest slanders
To stain my cousin with. One doth not know

How much an ill word may empoison liking.

URSULA

   O, do not do your cousin such a wrong!
   She cannot be so much without true judgement –
   Having so swift and excellent a wit
90   As she is prized to have – as to refuse
   So rare a gentleman as Signor Benedick.

HERO

   He is the only man of Italy,
   Always excepted my dear Claudio.

URSULA

   I pray you be not angry with me, madam,
   Speaking my fancy; Signor Benedick,
   For shape, for bearing, argument and valour,
   Goes foremost in report through Italy.

HERO

   Indeed, he hath an excellent good name.

URSULA

   His excellence did earn it ere he had it.
100   When are you married, madam?

HERO

   Why, every day, tomorrow. Come, go in;
   I'll show thee some attires, and have thy counsel
   Which is the best to furnish me tomorrow.

URSULA (to Hero)

   She's limed, I warrant you; we have caught her, madam.

HERO (to Ursula)

   If it prove so, then loving goes by haps;
   Some Cupid kills with arrows, some with traps.

                 Exeunt Hero and Ursula

BEATRICE (coming forward)

   What fire is in mine ears? Can this be true?
     Stand I condemned for pride and scorn so much?

Contempt, farewell! and maiden pride, adieu!
   No glory lives behind the back of such.   110
And, Benedick, love on; I will requite thee,
   Taming my wild heart to thy loving hand.
If thou dost love, my kindness shall incite thee
   To bind our loves up in a holy band.
For others say thou dost deserve, and I
Believe it better than reportingly.   *Exit*

Enter Don Pedro, Claudio, Benedick, and Leonato   **III.2**

DON PEDRO I do but stay till your marriage be consummate, and then go I toward Arragon.

CLAUDIO I'll bring you thither, my lord, if you'll vouchsafe me.

DON PEDRO Nay, that would be as great a soil in the new
gloss of your marriage as to show a child his new coat
and forbid him to wear it. I will only be bold with Benedick for his company; for, from the crown of his head
to the sole of his foot, he is all mirth; he hath twice or
thrice cut Cupid's bow-string and the little hangman   10
dare not shoot at him. He hath a heart as sound as a
bell and his tongue is the clapper, for what his heart
thinks, his tongue speaks.

BENEDICK Gallants, I am not as I have been.

LEONATO So say I; methinks you are sadder.

CLAUDIO I hope he be in love.

DON PEDRO Hang him, truant! There's no true drop of
blood in him to be truly touched with love; if he be sad,
he wants money.

BENEDICK I have the toothache.   20

DON PEDRO Draw it.

BENEDICK Hang it!

CLAUDIO You must hang it first, and draw it afterwards.

DON PEDRO What! Sigh for the toothache?

LEONATO Where is but a humour or a worm.

BENEDICK Well, everyone can master a grief but he that has it.

CLAUDIO Yet say I, he is in love.

DON PEDRO There is no appearance of fancy in him, unless it be a fancy that he hath to strange disguises; as to be a Dutchman today, a Frenchman tomorrow, or in the shape of two countries at once, as, a German from the waist downward, all slops, and a Spaniard from the hip upward, no doublet. Unless he have a fancy to this foolery, as it appears he hath, he is no fool for fancy, as you would have it appear he is.

CLAUDIO If he be not in love with some woman, there is no believing old signs. 'A brushes his hat o'mornings; what should that bode?

DON PEDRO Hath any man seen him at the barber's?

CLAUDIO No, but the barber's man hath been seen with him and the old ornament of his cheek hath already stuffed tennis-balls.

LEONATO Indeed, he looks younger than he did, by the loss of a beard.

DON PEDRO Nay, 'a rubs himself with civet; can you smell him out by that?

CLAUDIO That's as much as to say, the sweet youth's in love.

DON PEDRO The greatest note of it is his melancholy.

CLAUDIO And when was he wont to wash his face?

DON PEDRO Yea, or to paint himself? For the which, I hear what they say of him.

CLAUDIO Nay, but his jesting spirit, which is now crept into a lute-string and now governed by stops.

DON PEDRO Indeed, that tells a heavy tale for him; conclude, conclude he is in love.

CLAUDIO Nay, but I know who loves him.

DON PEDRO That would I know too; I warrant, one that
knows him not.   60

CLAUDIO Yes, and his ill conditions; and, in despite of all,
dies for him.

DON PEDRO She shall be buried with her face upwards.

BENEDICK Yet is this no charm for the toothache. Old
signor, walk aside with me; I have studied eight or nine
wise words to speak to you, which these hobby-horses
must not hear.   *Exeunt Benedick and Leonato*

DON PEDRO For my life, to break with him about Beatrice.

CLAUDIO 'Tis even so. Hero and Margaret have by this
played their parts with Beatrice, and then the two bears   70
will not bite one another when they meet.

   Enter Don John

DON JOHN My lord and brother, God save you!

DON PEDRO Good-e'en, brother.

DON JOHN If your leisure served, I would speak with you.

DON PEDRO In private?

DON JOHN If it please you; yet Count Claudio may hear,
for what I would speak of concerns him.

DON PEDRO What's the matter?

DON JOHN (*to Claudio*) Means your lordship to be
married tomorrow?   80

DON PEDRO You know he does.

DON JOHN I know not that, when he knows what I know.

CLAUDIO If there be any impediment, I pray you discover
it.

DON JOHN You may think I love you not; let that appear
hereafter, and aim better at me by that I now will
manifest. For my brother, I think he holds you well,
and in dearness of heart hath holp to effect your ensuing
marriage – surely suit ill spent, and labour ill bestowed!

DON PEDRO Why, what's the matter?   90

DON JOHN I came hither to tell you; and, circumstances
shortened, for she has been too long a talking of, the
lady is disloyal.

CLAUDIO Who, Hero?

DON JOHN Even she – Leonato's Hero, your Hero, every
man's Hero.

CLAUDIO Disloyal?

DON JOHN The word is too good to paint out her wicked-
ness. I could say she were worse; think you of a worse
title, and I will fit her to it. Wonder not till further
warrant. Go but with me tonight, you shall see her
chamber-window entered, even the night before her
wedding-day. If you love her then, tomorrow wed her;
but it would better fit your honour to change your mind.

CLAUDIO May this be so?

DON PEDRO I will not think it.

DON JOHN If you dare not trust that you see, confess not
that you know. If you will follow me, I will show you
enough; and when you have seen more and heard more,
proceed accordingly.

CLAUDIO If I see any thing tonight why I should not
marry her, tomorrow in the congregation, where I
should wed, there will I shame her.

DON PEDRO And, as I wooed for thee to obtain her, I will
join with thee to disgrace her.

DON JOHN I will disparage her no farther till you are my
witness; bear it coldly but till midnight, and let the
issue show itself.

DON PEDRO O day untowardly turned!

CLAUDIO O mischief strangely thwarting!

DON JOHN O plague right well prevented! So will you say
when you have seen the sequel.   *Exeunt*

Enter Dogberry and his compartner Verges with the   III.3
Watch

DOGBERRY Are you good men and true?

VERGES Yea, or else it were pity but they should suffer
salvation, body and soul.

DOGBERRY Nay, that were a punishment too good for
them, if they should have any allegiance in them, being
chosen for the Prince's watch.

VERGES Well, give them their charge, neighbour Dogberry.

DOGBERRY First, who think you the most desartless man
to be constable?   10

FIRST WATCHMAN Hugh Oatcake, sir, or George Seacoal,
for they can write and read.

DOGBERRY Come hither, neighbour Seacoal. God hath
blessed you with a good name. To be a well-favoured
man is the gift of fortune; but to write and read comes
by nature.

SECOND WATCHMAN Both which, Master Constable –

DOGBERRY You have; I knew it would be your answer.
Well, for your favour, sir, why, give God thanks, and
make no boast of it; and for your writing and reading,   20
let that appear when there is no need of such vanity. You
are thought here to be the most senseless and fit man
for the constable of the watch; therefore bear you the
lantern. This is your charge: you shall comprehend all
vagrom men; you are to bid any man stand, in the
Prince's name.

SECOND WATCHMAN How if 'a will not stand?

DOGBERRY Why, then, take no note of him, but let him go;
and presently call the rest of the watch together and
thank God you are rid of a knave.   30

VERGES If he will not stand when he is bidden, he is none
of the Prince's subjects.

DOGBERRY True, and they are to meddle with none but the Prince's subjects. You shall also make no noise in the streets; for for the watch to babble and to talk is most tolerable and not to be endured.

FIRST WATCHMAN We will rather sleep than talk; we know what belongs to a watch.

DOGBERRY Why, you speak like an ancient and most quiet
40   watchman, for I cannot see how sleeping should offend; only, have a care that your bills be not stolen. Well, you are to call at all the ale-houses, and bid those that are drunk get them to bed.

SECOND WATCHMAN How if they will not?

DOGBERRY Why, then, let them alone till they are sober; if they make you not then the better answer, you may say they are not the men you took them for.

SECOND WATCHMAN Well, sir.

DOGBERRY If you meet a thief, you may suspect him, by
50   virtue of your office, to be no true man; and, for such kind of men, the less you meddle or make with them, why, the more is for your honesty.

SECOND WATCHMAN If we know him to be a thief, shall we not lay hands on him?

DOGBERRY Truly, by your office, you may, but I think they that touch pitch will be defiled. The most peaceable way for you, if you do take a thief, is to let him show himself what he is and steal out of your company.

VERGES You have been always called a merciful man,
60   partner.

DOGBERRY Truly, I would not hang a dog by my will, much more a man who hath any honesty in him.

VERGES If you hear a child cry in the night, you must call to the nurse and bid her still it.

SECOND WATCHMAN How if the nurse be asleep and will not hear us?

DOGBERRY Why, then, depart in peace, and let the child
    wake her with crying; for the ewe that will not hear her
    lamb when it baes will never answer a calf when he
    bleats.   70
VERGES 'Tis very true.
DOGBERRY This is the end of the charge: you, constable,
    are to present the Prince's own person; if you meet the
    Prince in the night, you may stay him.
VERGES Nay, by'r Lady, that I think 'a cannot.
DOGBERRY Five shillings to one on't, with any man that
    knows the statutes, he may stay him; marry, not without
    the Prince be willing; for, indeed, the watch ought to
    offend no man, and it is an offence to stay a man against
    his will.   80
VERGES By'r Lady, I think it be so.
DOGBERRY Ha, ah ha! Well, masters, good night; an
    there be any matter of weight chances, call up me. Keep
    your fellows' counsels and your own, and good night.
    Come, neighbour.
FIRST WATCHMAN Well, masters, we hear our charge.
    Let us go sit here upon the church-bench till two, and
    then all to bed.
DOGBERRY One word more, honest neighbours. I pray
    you, watch about Signor Leonato's door, for the wed-   90
    ding being there tomorrow, there is a great coil to-night.
    Adieu; be vigitant, I beseech you.

                         Exeunt Dogberry and Verges
    Enter Borachio and Conrade
BORACHIO What, Conrade!
SECOND WATCHMAN (*aside*) Peace! stir not.
BORACHIO Conrade, I say!
CONRADE Here, man, I am at thy elbow.
BORACHIO Mass, and my elbow itched; I thought there
    would a scab follow.

CONRADE I will owe thee an answer for that; and now
forward with thy tale.

BORACHIO Stand thee close then under this pent-house,
for it drizzles rain; and I will, like a true drunkard,
utter all to thee.

SECOND WATCHMAN (*aside*) Some treason, masters; yet
stand close.

BORACHIO Therefore know I have earned of Don John a
thousand ducats.

CONRADE Is it possible that any villainy should be so dear?

BORACHIO Thou shouldst rather ask if it were possible
any villainy should be so rich; for when rich villains
have need of poor ones, poor ones may make what price
they will.

CONRADE I wonder at it.

BORACHIO That shows thou art unconfirmed. Thou
knowest that the fashion of a doublet, or a hat, or a
cloak, is nothing to a man.

CONRADE Yes, it is apparel.

BORACHIO I mean, the fashion.

CONRADE Yes, the fashion is the fashion.

BORACHIO Tush! I may as well say the fool's the fool. But
seest thou not what a deformed thief this fashion is?

FIRST WATCHMAN (*aside*) I know that Deformed; 'a has
been a vile thief this seven year; 'a goes up and down
like a gentleman. I remember his name.

BORACHIO Didst thou not hear somebody?

CONRADE No; 'twas the vane on the house.

BORACHIO Seest thou not, I say, what a deformed thief
this fashion is, how giddily 'a turns about all the hot
bloods between fourteen and five-and-thirty, sometimes fashioning them like Pharaoh's soldiers in the
reechy painting, sometime like god Bel's priests in the

old church-window, sometime like the shaven Hercules
in the smirched worm-eaten tapestry, where his codpiece seems as massy as his club?

CONRADE All this I see; and I see that the fashion wears
out more apparel than the man. But art not thou thyself
giddy with the fashion too, that thou hast shifted out
of thy tale into telling me of the fashion?

BORACHIO Not so, neither: but know that I have tonight
wooed Margaret, the Lady Hero's gentlewoman, by the   140
name of Hero; she leans me out at her mistress'
chamber-window, bids me a thousand times good-
night – I tell this tale vilely – I should first tell thee how
the Prince, Claudio, and my master, planted, and
placed, and possessed, by my master Don John, saw afar
off in the orchard this amiable encounter.

CONRADE And thought they Margaret was Hero?

BORACHIO Two of them did, the Prince and Claudio; but
the devil my master knew she was Margaret; and partly
by his oaths, which first possessed them, partly by the   150
dark night, which did deceive them, but chiefly by my
villainy, which did confirm any slander that Don John
had made, away went Claudio enraged; swore he would
meet her, as he was appointed, next morning at the
temple, and there, before the whole congregation, shame
her with what he saw o'er night, and send her home
again without a husband.

FIRST WATCHMAN We charge you, in the Prince's name,
stand!

SECOND WATCHMAN Call up the right Master Constable.   160
We have here recovered the most dangerous piece of
lechery that ever was known in the commonwealth.

FIRST WATCHMAN And one Deformed is one of them; I
know him, 'a wears a lock.

CONRADE Masters, masters –

SECOND WATCHMAN You'll be made bring Deformed
    forth, I warrant you.

CONRADE Masters –

FIRST WATCHMAN Never speak, we charge you; let us
170   obey you to go with us.

BORACHIO We are like to prove a goodly commodity,
    being taken up of these men's bills.

CONRADE A commodity in question, I warrant you. Come,
    we'll obey you.   *Exeunt*

III.4   *Enter Hero, and Margaret, and Ursula*

HERO Good Ursula, wake my cousin Beatrice, and desire
    her to rise.

URSULA I will, lady.

HERO And bid her come hither.

URSULA Well.   *Exit*

MARGARET Troth, I think your other rebato were better.

HERO No, pray thee, good Meg, I'll wear this.

MARGARET By my troth, 's not so good, and I warrant
    your cousin will say so.

10 HERO My cousin's a fool, and thou art another. I'll wear
    none but this.

MARGARET I like the new tire within excellently, if the
    hair were a thought browner; and your gown's a most
    rare fashion, i'faith. I saw the Duchess of Milan's gown
    that they praise so.

HERO O, that exceeds, they say.

MARGARET By my troth, 's but a nightgown in respect of
    yours – cloth o'gold, and cuts, and laced with silver, set
    with pearls, down-sleeves, side-sleeves, and skirts, round
20   underborne with a bluish tinsel; but for a fine, quaint,
    graceful and excellent fashion, yours is worth ten on't.

HERO God give me joy to wear it, for my heart is exceedingly heavy.

MARGARET 'Twill be heavier soon, by the weight of a man.

HERO Fie upon thee! Art not ashamed?

MARGARET Of what, lady? Of speaking honourably? Is
not marriage honourable in a beggar? Is not your lord
honourable without marriage? I think you would have
me say, 'saving your reverence, a husband'; an bad
thinking do not wrest true speaking, I'll offend nobody.   30
Is there any harm in 'the heavier for a husband'? None,
I think, an it be the right husband and the right wife;
otherwise 'tis light, and not heavy; ask my Lady
Beatrice else, here she comes.

Enter Beatrice

HERO Good morrow, coz.

BEATRICE Good morrow, sweet Hero.

HERO Why, how now? Do you speak in the sick tune?

BEATRICE I am out of all other tune, methinks.

MARGARET Clap's into 'Light o' love'; that goes without a
burden. Do you sing it, and I'll dance it.   40

BEATRICE Ye light o' love, with your heels! Then if your
husband have stables enough, you'll see he shall lack no
barnes.

MARGARET O illegitimate construction! I scorn that with
my heels.

BEATRICE 'Tis almost five o'clock, cousin; 'tis time you
were ready. By my troth, I am exceeding ill; heigh-ho!

MARGARET For a hawk, a horse, or a husband?

BEATRICE For the letter that begins them all, H.

MARGARET Well, an you be not turned Turk, there's no   50
more sailing by the star.

BEATRICE What means the fool, trow?

MARGARET Nothing I; but God send everyone their
heart's desire!

HERO These gloves the Count sent me; they are an excellent perfume.

BEATRICE I am stuffed, cousin, I cannot smell.

MARGARET A maid, and stuffed! There's goodly catching of cold.

60 BEATRICE O, God help me! God help me! How long have you professed apprehension?

MARGARET Ever since you left it. Doth not my wit become me rarely?

BEATRICE It is not seen enough; you should wear it in your cap. By my troth, I am sick.

MARGARET Get you some of this distilled Carduus Benedictus, and lay it to your heart: it is the only thing for a qualm.

HERO There thou prickest her with a thistle.

70 BEATRICE Benedictus! Why Benedictus? You have some moral in this Benedictus.

MARGARET Moral? No, by my troth, I have no moral meaning; I meant plain holy-thistle. You may think perchance that I think you are in love. Nay, by'r Lady, I am not such a fool to think what I list, nor I list not to think what I can, nor indeed I cannot think, if I would think my heart out of thinking, that you are in love, or that you will be in love, or that you can be in love. Yet Benedick was such another, and now is he become a

80 man; he swore he would never marry, and yet now, in despite of his heart, he eats his meat without grudging; and how you may be converted I know not, but methinks you look with your eyes as other women do.

BEATRICE What pace is this that thy tongue keeps?

MARGARET Not a false gallop.

    Enter Ursula

URSULA Madam, withdraw; the Prince, the Count, Signor

Benedick, Don John, and all the gallants of the town, are
come to fetch you to church.

HERO Help to dress me, good coz, good Meg, good
Ursula.   *Exeunt*   90

Enter Leonato, with the Constable, Dogberry and the   III.5
Headborough, Verges

LEONATO What would you with me, honest neighbour?

DOGBERRY Marry, sir, I would have some confidence with
you that decerns you nearly.

LEONATO Brief, I pray you, for you see it is a busy time
with me.

DOGBERRY Marry, this it is, sir.

VERGES Yes, in truth it is, sir.

LEONATO What is it, my good friends?

DOGBERRY Goodman Verges, sir, speaks a little off the
matter – an old man, sir, and his wits are not so blunt as,   10
God help, I would desire they were; but, in faith, honest
as the skin between his brows.

VERGES Yes, I thank God I am as honest as any man living
that is an old man and no honester than I.

DOGBERRY Comparisons are odorous; *palabras*, neighbour
Verges.

LEONATO Neighbours, you are tedious.

DOGBERRY It pleases your worship to say so, but we are
the poor Duke's officers; but truly, for mine own part, if
I were as tedious as a king, I could find it in my heart to   20
bestow it all of your worship.

LEONATO All thy tediousness on me, ah?

DOGBERRY Yea, an't 'twere a thousand pound more than
'tis, for I hear as good exclamation on your worship as
of any man in the city; and though I be but a poor man,
I am glad to hear it.

VERGES And so am I.

LEONATO I would fain know what you have to say.

VERGES Marry, sir, our watch tonight, excepting your
worship's presence, ha' ta'en a couple of as arrant knaves
as any in Messina.

DOGBERRY A good old man, sir, he will be talking; as they
say, 'When the age is in, the wit is out.' God help us, it is
a world to see! Well said, i'faith, neighbour Verges;
well, God's a good man; an two men ride of a horse, one
must ride behind. An honest soul, i'faith, sir, by my
troth he is, as ever broke bread. But God is to be wor-
shipped; all men are not alike. Alas, good neighbour!

LEONATO Indeed, neighbour, he comes too short of you.

DOGBERRY Gifts that God gives.

LEONATO I must leave you.

DOGBERRY One word, sir: our watch, sir, have indeed
comprehended two aspicious persons, and we would
have them this morning examined before your worship.

LEONATO Take their examination yourself and bring it
me; I am now in great haste, as it may appear unto you.

DOGBERRY It shall be suffigance.

LEONATO Drink some wine ere you go. Fare you well.

Enter a Messenger

MESSENGER My lord, they stay for you to give your
daughter to her husband.

LEONATO I'll wait upon them; I am ready.

Exeunt Leonato and Messenger

DOGBERRY Go, good partner, go, get you to Francis Seacoal; bid him bring his pen and inkhorn to the gaol.
We are now to examination these men.

VERGES And we must do it wisely.

DOGBERRY We will spare for no wit, I warrant you. Here's
that shall drive some of them to a non-come; only get

the learned writer to set down our excommunication,
and meet me at the gaol.   *Exeunt*

*

Enter Don Pedro, Don John, Leonato, Friar Francis,   IV.1
Claudio, Benedick, Hero, Beatrice, and attendants

LEONATO Come, Friar Francis, be brief; only to the plain
form of marriage, and you shall recount their particular
duties afterwards.

FRIAR You come hither, my lord, to marry this lady?

CLAUDIO No.

LEONATO To be married to her; Friar, you come to marry
her!

FRIAR Lady, you come hither to be married to this Count?

HERO I do.

FRIAR If either of you know any inward impediment why   10
you should not be conjoined, I charge you, on your souls,
to utter it.

CLAUDIO Know you any, Hero?

HERO None, my lord.

FRIAR Know you any, Count?

LEONATO I dare make his answer, None.

CLAUDIO O, what men dare do! What men may do!
What men daily do, not knowing what they do!

BENEDICK How now! Interjections? Why, then, some be
of laughing, as, ah, ha, he!   20

CLAUDIO
Stand thee by, Friar. Father, by your leave:
Will you with free and unconstrainèd soul
Give me this maid, your daughter?

LEONATO
As freely, son, as God did give her me.

CLAUDIO

And what have I to give you back, whose worth
May counterpoise this rich and precious gift?

DON PEDRO

Nothing, unless you render her again.

CLAUDIO

Sweet Prince, you learn me noble thankfulness.
There, Leonato, take her back again,
30   Give not this rotten orange to your friend;
She's but the sign and semblance of her honour.
Behold how like a maid she blushes here!
O, what authority and show of truth
Can cunning sin cover itself withal!
Comes not that blood as modest evidence
To witness simple virtue? Would you not swear,
All you that see her, that she were a maid
By these exterior shows? But she is none;
She knows the heat of a luxurious bed.
40   Her blush is guiltiness, not modesty.

LEONATO

What do you mean, my lord?

CLAUDIO   Not to be married,
Not to knit my soul to an approvèd wanton.

LEONATO

Dear my lord, if you, in your own proof,
Have vanquished the resistance of her youth,
And made defeat of her virginity –

CLAUDIO

I know what you would say. If I have known her,
You will say she did embrace me as a husband,
And so extenuate the 'forehand sin.
No, Leonato,
50   I never tempted her with word too large,
But, as a brother to his sister, showed

Bashful sincerity and comely love.

HERO

And seemed I ever otherwise to you?

CLAUDIO

Out on thee! Seeming! I will write against it.
You seem to me as Dian in her orb,
As chaste as is the bud ere it be blown;
But you are more intemperate in your blood
Than Venus, or those pampered animals
That rage in savage sensuality.

HERO

Is my lord well, that he doth speak so wide?   60

LEONATO

Sweet Prince, why speak not you?

DON PEDRO   What should I speak?
I stand dishonoured, that have gone about
To link my dear friend to a common stale.

LEONATO

Are these things spoken, or do I but dream?

DON JOHN

Sir, they are spoken, and these things are true.

BENEDICK

This looks not like a nuptial.

HERO   True? O God!

CLAUDIO

Leonato, stand I here?
Is this the Prince? Is this the Prince's brother?
Is this face Hero's? Are our eyes our own?

LEONATO

All this is so; but what of this, my lord?   70

CLAUDIO

Let me but move one question to your daughter;
And, by that fatherly and kindly power
That you have in her, bid her answer truly.

LEONATO

 I charge thee do so, as thou art my child.

HERO

 O God defend me! How am I beset!

 What kind of catechizing call you this?

CLAUDIO

 To make you answer truly to your name.

HERO

 Is it not Hero? Who can blot that name

 With any just reproach?

CLAUDIO   Marry, that can Hero;

80 Hero itself can blot out Hero's virtue.

 What man was he talked with you yesternight

 Out at your window betwixt twelve and one?

 Now, if you are a maid, answer to this.

HERO

 I talked with no man at that hour, my lord.

DON PEDRO

 Why, then are you no maiden. Leonato,

 I am sorry you must hear. Upon mine honour,

 Myself, my brother, and this grievèd Count

 Did see her, hear her, at that hour last night

 Talk with a ruffian at her chamber-window;

90 Who hath, indeed, most like a liberal villain,

 Confessed the vile encounters they have had

 A thousand times in secret.

DON JOHN

 Fie, fie, they are not to be named, my lord,

 Not to be spoke of!

 There is not chastity enough in language

 Without offence to utter them. Thus, pretty lady,

 I am sorry for thy much misgovernment.

CLAUDIO

 O Hero! What a Hero hadst thou been,

If half thy outward graces had been placed
About thy thoughts and counsels of thy heart!   100
But fare thee well, most foul, most fair! Farewell,
Thou pure impiety and impious purity!
For thee I'll lock up all the gates of love,
And on my eyelids shall conjecture hang,
To turn all beauty into thoughts of harm,
And never shall it more be gracious.

LEONATO
Hath no man's dagger here a point for me?

Hero swoons

BEATRICE
Why, how now, cousin! Wherefore sink you down?

DON JOHN
Come, let us go. These things, come thus to light,
Smother her spirits up.   110

Exeunt Don Pedro, Don John, and Claudio

BENEDICK
How doth the lady?

BEATRICE   Dead, I think. Help, uncle!
Hero! Why, Hero! Uncle! Signor Benedick! Friar!

LEONATO
O Fate! Take not away thy heavy hand.
Death is the fairest cover for her shame
That may be wished for.

BEATRICE   How now, cousin Hero?

FRIAR
Have comfort, lady.

LEONATO
Dost thou look up?

FRIAR   Yea, wherefore should she not?

LEONATO
Wherefore! Why, doth not every earthly thing
Cry shame upon her? Could she here deny

120 The story that is printed in her blood?
Do not live, Hero, do not ope thine eyes;
For, did I think thou wouldst not quickly die,
Thought I thy spirits were stronger than thy shames,
Myself would, on the rearward of reproaches,
Strike at thy life. Grieved I, I had but one?
Chid I for that at frugal Nature's frame?
O, one too much by thee! Why had I one?
Why ever wast thou lovely in my eyes?
Why had I not with charitable hand
130 Took up a beggar's issue at my gates,
Who smirchèd thus and mired with infamy,
I might have said 'No part of it is mine;
This shame derives itself from unknown loins'?
But mine and mine I loved and mine I praised
And mine that I was proud on, mine so much
That I myself was to myself not mine,
Valuing of her — why, she, O, she is fallen
Into a pit of ink, that the wide sea
Hath drops too few to wash her clean again
140 And salt too little which may season give
To her foul tainted flesh!

BENEDICK   Sir, sir, be patient.
For my part, I am so attired in wonder,
I know not what to say.

BEATRICE
O, on my soul, my cousin is belied!

BENEDICK
Lady, were you her bedfellow last night?

BEATRICE
No, truly not; although, until last night,
I have this twelvemonth been her bedfellow.

LEONATO
Confirmed, confirmed! O, that is stronger made

Which was before barred up with ribs of iron!
Would the two Princes lie, and Claudio lie,   150
Who loved her so, that, speaking of her foulness,
Washed it with tears? Hence from her, let her die!

FRIAR
    Hear me a little;
    For I have only silent been so long,
    And given way unto this course of fortune
    By noting of the lady. I have marked
    A thousand blushing apparitions
    To start into her face, a thousand innocent shames
    In angel whiteness beat away those blushes;
    And in her eye there hath appeared a fire,   160
    To burn the errors that these Princes hold
    Against her maiden truth. Call me a fool;
    Trust not my reading nor my observations,
    Which with experimental seal doth warrant
    The tenor of my book; trust not my age,
    My reverence, calling, nor divinity,
    If this sweet lady lie not guiltless here
    Under some biting error.

LEONATO   Friar, it cannot be.
    Thou seest that all the grace that she hath left
    Is that she will not add to her damnation   170
    A sin of perjury; she not denies it:
    Why seek'st thou then to cover with excuse
    That which appears in proper nakedness?

FRIAR
    Lady, what man is he you are accused of?

HERO
    They know that do accuse me; I know none.
    If I know more of any man alive
    Than that which maiden modesty doth warrant,
    Let all my sins lack mercy! O my father,

Prove you that any man with me conversed
180   At hours unmeet, or that I yesternight
Maintained the change of words with any creature,
Refuse me, hate me, torture me to death!

FRIAR

There is some strange misprision in the Princes.

BENEDICK

Two of them have the very bent of honour;
And if their wisdoms be misled in this,
The practice of it lives in John the Bastard,
Whose spirits toil in frame of villainies.

LEONATO

I know not. If they speak but truth of her,
These hands shall tear her; if they wrong her honour,
190   The proudest of them shall well hear of it.
Time hath not yet so dried this blood of mine,
Nor age so eat up my invention,
Nor fortune made such havoc of my means,
Nor my bad life reft me so much of friends,
But they shall find, awaked in such a kind,
Both strength of limb and policy of mind,
Ability in means and choice of friends
To quit me of them throughly.

FRIAR   Pause awhile,
And let my counsel sway you in this case.
200   Your daughter here the Princes left for dead;
Let her awhile be secretly kept in,
And publish it that she is dead indeed.
Maintain a mourning ostentation,
And on your family's old monument
Hang mournful epitaphs and do all rites
That appertain unto a burial.

LEONATO

What shall become of this? What will this do?

FRIAR

    Marry, this, well carried, shall on her behalf
    Change slander to remorse; that is some good.
    But not for that dream I on this strange course,   210
    But on this travail look for greater birth.
    She dying, as it must be so maintained,
    Upon the instant that she was accused,
    Shall be lamented, pitied, and excused
    Of every hearer; for it so falls out
    That what we have we prize not to the worth
    Whiles we enjoy it, but being lacked and lost,
    Why, then we rack the value, then we find
    The virtue that possession would not show us
    Whiles it was ours. So will it fare with Claudio.   220
    When he shall hear she died upon his words,
    Th'idea of her life shall sweetly creep
    Into his study of imagination,
    And every lovely organ of her life
    Shall come apparelled in more precious habit,
    More moving, delicate, and full of life,
    Into the eye and prospect of his soul,
    Than when she lived indeed. Then shall he mourn,
    If ever love had interest in his liver,
    And wish he had not so accusèd her –   230
    No, though he thought his accusation true.
    Let this be so, and doubt not but success
    Will fashion the event in better shape
    Than I can lay it down in likelihood.
    But if all aim but this be levelled false,
    The supposition of the lady's death
    Will quench the wonder of her infamy;
    And if it sort not well, you may conceal her,
    As best befits her wounded reputation,
    In some reclusive and religious life,   240

Out of all eyes, tongues, minds, and injuries.

BENEDICK
Signor Leonato, let the Friar advise you;
And though you know my inwardness and love
Is very much unto the Prince and Claudio,
Yet, by mine honour, I will deal in this
As secretly and justly as your soul
Should with your body.

LEONATO   Being that I flow in grief,
The smallest twine may lead me.

FRIAR
'Tis well consented. Presently away;
250   For to strange sores strangely they strain the cure.
Come, lady, die to live; this wedding-day
Perhaps is but prolonged; have patience and endure.

Exeunt all but Benedick and Beatrice

BENEDICK Lady Beatrice, have you wept all this while?

BEATRICE Yea, and I will weep a while longer.

BENEDICK I will not desire that.

BEATRICE You have no reason; I do it freely.

BENEDICK Surely I do believe your fair cousin is wronged.

BEATRICE Ah, how much might the man deserve of me
that would right her!

260   BENEDICK Is there any way to show such friendship?

BEATRICE A very even way, but no such friend.

BENEDICK May a man do it?

BEATRICE It is a man's office, but not yours.

BENEDICK I do love nothing in the world so well as you; is
not that strange?

BEATRICE As strange as the thing I know not. It were as
possible for me to say I loved nothing so well as you; but
believe me not, and yet I lie not; I confess nothing, nor I
deny nothing. I am sorry for my cousin.

270   BENEDICK By my sword, Beatrice, thou lovest me.

BEATRICE Do not swear, and eat it.

BENEDICK I will swear by it that you love me; and I will make him eat it that says I love not you.

BEATRICE Will you not eat your word?

BENEDICK With no sauce that can be devised to it; I protest I love thee.

BEATRICE Why, then, God forgive me!

BENEDICK What offence, sweet Beatrice?

BEATRICE You have stayed me in a happy hour; I was about to protest I loved you.   280

BENEDICK And do it with all thy heart.

BEATRICE I love you with so much of my heart that none is left to protest.

BENEDICK Come, bid me do anything for thee.

BEATRICE Kill Claudio.

BENEDICK Ha! Not for the wide world.

BEATRICE You kill me to deny it. Farewell.

BENEDICK (taking her by the hand) Tarry, sweet Beatrice.

BEATRICE I am gone though I am here; there is no love in you. Nay, I pray you, let me go.   290

BENEDICK Beatrice –

BEATRICE In faith, I will go.

BENEDICK We'll be friends first.

BEATRICE You dare easier be friends with me than fight with mine enemy.

BENEDICK Is Claudio thine enemy?

BEATRICE Is he not approved in the height a villain that hath slandered, scorned, dishonoured my kinswoman? O that I were a man! What, bear her in hand until they come to take hands, and then, with public accusation,   300 uncovered slander, unmitigated rancour – O God, that I were a man! I would eat his heart in the market-place.

BENEDICK Hear me, Beatrice –

BEATRICE Talk with a man out at a window! A proper saying!

BENEDICK Nay, but Beatrice –

BEATRICE Sweet Hero! She is wronged, she is slandered, she is undone.

BENEDICK Beat –

310 BEATRICE Princes and counties! Surely, a princely testimony, a goodly count, Count Comfect; a sweet gallant, surely! O that I were a man for his sake, or that I had any friend would be a man for my sake! But manhood is melted into curtsies, valour into compliment, and men are only turned into tongue, and trim ones too. He is now as valiant as Hercules that only tells a lie and swears it. I cannot be a man with wishing, therefore I will die a woman with grieving.

BENEDICK Tarry, good Beatrice. By this hand, I love 320 thee.

BEATRICE Use it for my love some other way than swearing by it.

BENEDICK Think you in your soul the Count Claudio hath wronged Hero?

BEATRICE Yea, as sure as I have a thought or a soul.

BENEDICK Enough, I am engaged; I will challenge him. I will kiss your hand, and so I leave you. By this hand, Claudio shall render me a dear account. As you hear of me, so think of me. Go, comfort your cousin; I must say 330 she is dead; and so, farewell.   *Exeunt*

IV.2   *Enter Dogberry, Verges, and the Sexton in gowns;*
          and the Watch, with Conrade and Borachio

DOGBERRY Is our whole dissembly appeared?

VERGES O, a stool and a cushion for the Sexton.

SEXTON Which be the malefactors?

DOGBERRY Marry, that am I and my partner.

VERGES Nay, that's certain; we have the exhibition to examine.

SEXTON But which are the offenders that are to be ex-
    amined? Let them come before Master Constable.

DOGBERRY Yea, marry, let them come before me. What is
    your name, friend?   10

BORACHIO Borachio.

DOGBERRY Pray, write down, Borachio. Yours, sirrah?

CONRADE I am a gentleman, sir, and my name is
    Conrade.

DOGBERRY Write down Master Gentleman Conrade.
    Masters, do you serve God?

CONRADE *and* BORACHIO Yea, sir, we hope.

DOGBERRY Write down, that they hope they serve God —
    and write God first, for God defend but God should go
    before such villains! Masters, it is proved already that   20
    you are little better than false knaves, and it will go near
    to be thought so shortly. How answer you for your-
    selves?

CONRADE Marry, sir, we say we are none.

DOGBERRY A marvellous witty fellow, I assure you; but
    I will go about with him. Come you hither, sirrah; a
    word in your ear. Sir, I say to you, it is thought you are
    false knaves.

BORACHIO Sir, I say to you we are none.

DOGBERRY Well, stand aside. 'Fore God, they are both in   30
    a tale. Have you writ down that they are none?

SEXTON Master Constable, you go not the way to examine;
    you must call forth the watch that are their accusers.

DOGBERRY Yea, marry, that's the eftest way; let the watch
    come forth. Masters, I charge you in the Prince's name,
    accuse these men.

FIRST WATCHMAN This man said, sir, that Don John,
    the Prince's brother, was a villain.

DOGBERRY Write down Prince John a villain. Why, this is
    flat perjury, to call a Prince's brother villain.   40

BORACHIO Master Constable —

DOGBERRY Pray thee, fellow, peace; I do not like thy
    look, I promise thee.

SEXTON What heard you him say else?

SECOND WATCHMAN Marry, that he had received a
    thousand ducats of Don John for accusing the Lady
    Hero wrongfully.

DOGBERRY Flat burglary as ever was committed.

VERGES Yea, by mass, that it is.

50 SEXTON What else, fellow?

FIRST WATCHMAN And that Count Claudio did mean,
    upon his words, to disgrace Hero before the whole
    assembly, and not marry her.

DOGBERRY O villain! Thou wilt be condemned into ever-
    lasting redemption for this.

SEXTON What else?

SECOND WATCHMAN This is all.

SEXTON And this is more, masters, than you can deny.
    Prince John is this morning secretly stolen away; Hero
60 was in this manner accused, in this very manner refused,
    and upon the grief of this suddenly died. Master Con-
    stable, let these men be bound, and brought to Leo-
    nato's; I will go before and show him their examina-
    tion.   *Exit*

DOGBERRY Come, let them be opinioned.

VERGES Let them be — in the hands.

CONRADE Off, coxcomb!

DOGBERRY God's my life, where's the Sexton? Let him
    write down the Prince's officer coxcomb. Come, bind
70 them. Thou naughty varlet!

CONRADE Away! You are an ass, you are an ass.

DOGBERRY Dost thou not suspect my place? Dost thou
    not suspect my years? O that he were here to write me
    down an ass! But, masters, remember that I am an ass;

though it be not written down, yet forget not that I am
an ass. No, thou villain, thou art full of piety, as shall be
proved upon thee by good witness. I am a wise fellow,
and, which is more, an officer; and, which is more, a
householder; and, which is more, as pretty a piece of
flesh as any is in Messina; and one that knows the law,   80
go to; and a rich fellow enough, go to; and a fellow that
hath had losses; and one that hath two gowns and everything handsome about him. Bring him away. O that I
had been writ down an ass!   *Exeunt*

                              *

Enter Leonato and his brother Antonio   V.I

ANTONIO
    If you go on thus, you will kill yourself;
    And 'tis not wisdom thus to second grief
    Against yourself.
LEONATO   I pray thee, cease thy counsel,
    Which falls into mine ears as profitless
    As water in a sieve. Give not me counsel,
    Nor let no comforter delight mine ear
    But such a one whose wrongs do suit with mine.
    Bring me a father that so loved his child,
    Whose joy of her is overwhelmed like mine,
    And bid him speak of patience;   10
    Measure his woe the length and breadth of mine,
    And let it answer every strain for strain,
    And thus for thus, and such a grief for such,
    In every lineament, branch, shape, and form;
    If such a one will smile and stroke his beard,
    And, sorry wag, cry 'hem!' when he should groan,
    Patch grief with proverbs, make misfortune drunk

With candle-wasters – bring him yet to me,
And I of him will gather patience.
20   But there is no such man; for, brother, men
Can counsel and speak comfort to that grief
Which they themselves not feel; but, tasting it,
Their counsel turns to passion, which before
Would give preceptial medicine to rage,
Fetter strong madness in a silken thread,
Charm ache with air and agony with words.
No, no; 'tis all men's office to speak patience
To those that wring under the load of sorrow,
But no man's virtue nor sufficiency
30   To be so moral when he shall endure
The like himself. Therefore give me no counsel;
My griefs cry louder than advertisement.

ANTONIO
Therein do men from children nothing differ.

LEONATO
I pray thee, peace. I will be flesh and blood;
For there was never yet philosopher
That could endure the toothache patiently,
However they have writ the style of gods,
And made a push at chance and sufferance.

ANTONIO
Yet bend not all the harm upon yourself;
40   Make those that do offend you suffer too.

LEONATO
There thou speak'st reason; nay, I will do so.
My soul doth tell me Hero is belied,
And that shall Claudio know; so shall the Prince,
And all of them that thus dishonour her.

ANTONIO
Here comes the Prince and Claudio hastily.
    Enter Don Pedro and Claudio

DON PEDRO
Good-e'en, good-e'en.

CLAUDIO   Good day to both of you.

LEONATO
Hear you, my lords!

DON PEDRO   We have some haste, Leonato.

LEONATO
Some haste, my lord! Well, fare you well, my lord;
Are you so hasty now? Well, all is one.

DON PEDRO
Nay, do not quarrel with us, good old man.   50

ANTONIO
If he could right himself with quarrelling,
Some of us would lie low.

CLAUDIO   Who wrongs him?

LEONATO
Marry, thou dost wrong me, thou dissembler, thou!
— Nay, never lay thy hand upon thy sword;
I fear thee not.

CLAUDIO   Marry, beshrew my hand,
If it should give your age such cause of fear:
In faith, my hand meant nothing to my sword.

LEONATO
Tush, tush, man, never fleer and jest at me;
I speak not like a dotard nor a fool,
As under privilege of age to brag   60
What I have done being young, or what would do
Were I not old. Know, Claudio, to thy head,
Thou hast so wronged mine innocent child and me
That I am forced to lay my reverence by,
And with grey hairs and bruise of many days,
Do challenge thee to trial of a man.
I say thou hast belied mine innocent child.
Thy slander hath gone through and through her heart,

And she lies buried with her ancestors –
70   O, in a tomb where never scandal slept,
      Save this of hers, framed by thy villainy!

CLAUDIO
  My villainy?

LEONATO   Thine, Claudio; thine, I say.

DON PEDRO
  You say not right, old man.

LEONATO   My lord, my lord,
      I'll prove it on his body if he dare,
      Despite his nice fence and his active practice,
      His May of youth and bloom of lustihood.

CLAUDIO
  Away! I will not have to do with you.

LEONATO
  Canst thou so daff me? Thou hast killed my child;
  If thou kill'st me, boy, thou shalt kill a man.

ANTONIO
80   He shall kill two of us, and men indeed;
      But that's no matter, let him kill one first.
      Win me and wear me; let him answer me.
      Come, follow me, boy; come, sir boy, come, follow me;
      Sir boy, I'll whip you from your foining fence;
      Nay, as I am a gentleman, I will.

LEONATO
  Brother –

ANTONIO
  Content yourself. God knows I loved my niece;
  And she is dead, slandered to death by villains,
  That dare as well answer a man indeed
90   As I dare take a serpent by the tongue.
      Boys, apes, braggarts, Jacks, milksops!

LEONATO   Brother Antony –

ANTONIO
Hold you content. What, man! I know them, yea,
And what they weigh, even to the utmost scruple –
Scambling, out-facing, fashion-monging boys,
That lie and cog and flout, deprave and slander,
Go anticly, show outward hideousness,
And speak off half a dozen dangerous words,
How they might hurt their enemies, if they durst;
And this is all.

LEONATO
But, brother Antony –

ANTONIO   Come, 'tis no matter;   100
Do not you meddle, let me deal in this.

DON PEDRO
Gentlemen both, we will not wake your patience.
My heart is sorry for your daughter's death,
But, on my honour, she was charged with nothing
But what was true and very full of proof.

LEONATO
My lord, my lord –

DON PEDRO   I will not hear you.

LEONATO   No?
Come brother, away. I will be heard.

ANTONIO
And shall, or some of us will smart for it.
                              Exeunt Leonato and Antonio

DON PEDRO
See, see; here comes the man we went to seek.
    Enter Benedick

CLAUDIO Now, signor, what news?   110
BENEDICK Good day, my lord.
DON PEDRO Welcome, signor; you are almost come to
    part almost a fray.

CLAUDIO We had like to have had our two noses snapped
    off with two old men without teeth.

DON PEDRO Leonato and his brother. What think'st thou?
    Had we fought, I doubt we should have been too young
    for them.

BENEDICK In a false quarrel there is no true valour. I
120   came to seek you both.

CLAUDIO We have been up and down to seek thee, for we
    are high-proof melancholy, and would fain have it
    beaten away. Wilt thou use thy wit?

BENEDICK It is in my scabbard; shall I draw it?

DON PEDRO Dost thou wear thy wit by thy side?

CLAUDIO Never any did so, though very many have been
    beside their wit. I will bid thee draw, as we do the
    minstrels – draw to pleasure us.

DON PEDRO As I am an honest man, he looks pale.
130   Art thou sick, or angry?

CLAUDIO What, courage, man! What though care killed
    a cat, thou hast mettle enough in thee to kill care.

BENEDICK Sir, I shall meet your wit in the career, an you
    charge it against me. I pray you choose another subject.

CLAUDIO Nay, then, give him another staff; this last was
    broke cross.

DON PEDRO By this light, he changes more and more; I
    think he be angry indeed.

CLAUDIO If he be, he knows how to turn his girdle.

140 BENEDICK Shall I speak a word in your ear?

CLAUDIO God bless me from a challenge!

BENEDICK (aside to Claudio) You are a villain; I jest not.
    I will make it good how you dare, with what you dare,
    and when you dare. Do me right, or I will protest your
    cowardice. You have killed a sweet lady, and her death
    shall fall heavy on you. Let me hear from you.

CLAUDIO Well, I will meet you, so I may have good cheer.

DON PEDRO What, a feast, a feast?

CLAUDIO I'faith, I thank him; he hath bid me to a calf's
head and a capon, the which if I do not carve most   150
curiously, say my knife's naught. Shall I not find a
woodcock too?

BENEDICK Sir, your wit ambles well; it goes easily.

DON PEDRO I'll tell thee how Beatrice praised thy wit the
other day. I said, thou hadst a fine wit. 'True,' said she,
'a fine little one.' 'No,' said I, 'a great wit.' 'Right,' says
she, 'a great gross one.' 'Nay,' said I, 'a good wit.' 'Just,'
said she, 'it hurts nobody.' 'Nay,' said I, 'the gentleman
is wise.' 'Certain,' said she, 'a wise gentleman.' 'Nay,'
said I, 'he hath the tongues.' 'That I believe,' said she,   160
'for he swore a thing to me on Monday night, which he
forswore on Tuesday morning. There's a double
tongue; there's two tongues.' Thus did she, an hour
together, trans-shape thy particular virtues; yet at last
she concluded with a sigh, thou wast the properest man
in Italy.

CLAUDIO For the which she wept heartily, and said she
cared not.

DON PEDRO Yea, that she did; but yet, for all that, an if
she did not hate him deadly, she would love him dearly.   170
The old man's daughter told us all.

CLAUDIO All, all; and, moreover, God saw him when he
was hid in the garden.

DON PEDRO But when shall we set the savage bull's
horns on the sensible Benedick's head?

CLAUDIO Yes, and text underneath, 'Here dwells Benedick, the married man'?

BENEDICK Fare you well, boy; you know my mind. I will
leave you now to your gossip-like humour; you break
jests as braggarts do their blades, which, God be   180
thanked, hurt not. (*To Don Pedro*) My lord, for your

many courtesies I thank you; I must discontinue your
company. Your brother the Bastard is fled from
Messina. You have among you killed a sweet and innocent lady. For my Lord Lackbeard there, he and I shall
meet; and till then, peace be with him.   *Exit*

DON PEDRO He is in earnest.

CLAUDIO In most profound earnest; and, I'll warrant
you, for the love of Beatrice.

190 DON PEDRO And hath challenged thee.

CLAUDIO Most sincerely.

DON PEDRO What a pretty thing man is when he goes in
his doublet and hose and leaves off his wit!

CLAUDIO He is then a giant to an ape; but then is an ape
a doctor to such a man.

DON PEDRO But, soft you, let me be; pluck up, my heart,
and be sad. Did he not say, my brother was fled?

*Enter Dogberry, Verges, Watch, Conrade, and
Borachio*

DOGBERRY Come, you, sir; if justice cannot tame you, she
shall ne'er weigh more reasons in her balance. Nay, an
200 you be a cursing hypocrite once, you must be looked to.

DON PEDRO How now, two of my brother's men bound?
Borachio one!

CLAUDIO Hearken after their offence, my lord.

DON PEDRO Officers, what offence have these men done?

DOGBERRY Marry, sir, they have committed false report;
moreover they have spoken untruths; secondarily, they
are slanders; sixth and lastly, they have belied a lady;
thirdly, they have verified unjust things; and, to conclude, they are lying knaves.

210 DON PEDRO First, I ask thee what they have done; thirdly,
I ask thee what's their offence; sixth and lastly, why
they are committed; and, to conclude, what you lay to
their charge.

CLAUDIO Rightly reasoned, and in his own division; and,
 by my troth, there's one meaning well suited.

DON PEDRO Who have you offended, masters, that you
 are thus bound to your answer? This learned Constable
 is too cunning to be understood; what's your offence?

BORACHIO Sweet Prince, let me go no farther to mine
 answer; do you hear me, and let this Count kill me. I   220
 have deceived even your very eyes: what your wisdoms
 could not discover, these shallow fools have brought to
 light; who in the night overheard me confessing to this
 man how Don John your brother incensed me to slander
 the Lady Hero; how you were brought into the orchard
 and saw me court Margaret in Hero's garments; how
 you disgraced her, when you should marry her. My villainy they have upon record, which I had rather seal
 with my death than repeat over to my shame. The lady
 is dead upon mine and my master's false accusation; and,   230
 briefly, I desire nothing but the reward of a villain.

DON PEDRO
 Runs not this speech like iron through your blood?

CLAUDIO
 I have drunk poison whiles he uttered it.

DON PEDRO
 But did my brother set thee on to this?

BORACHIO
 Yes, and paid me richly for the practice of it.

DON PEDRO
 He is composed and framed of treachery,
 And fled he is upon this villainy.

CLAUDIO
 Sweet Hero, now thy image doth appear
 In the rare semblance that I loved it first.

DOGBERRY Come, bring away the plaintiffs; by this time   240
 our Sexton hath reformed Signor Leonato of the matter.

And, masters, do not forget to specify, when time and
place shall serve, that I am an ass.

VERGES Here, here comes master Signor Leonato, and
the Sexton too.

Enter Leonato and Antonio, with the Sexton

LEONATO

Which is the villain? Let me see his eyes,
That, when I note another man like him,
I may avoid him. Which of these is he?

BORACHIO

If you would know your wronger, look on me.

LEONATO

250   Art thou the slave that with thy breath hast killed
Mine innocent child?

BORACHIO   Yea, even I alone.

LEONATO

No, not so, villain, thou beliest thyself –
Here stand a pair of honourable men,
A third is fled, that had a hand in it.
I thank you, Princes, for my daughter's death;
Record it with your high and worthy deeds.
'Twas bravely done, if you bethink you of it.

CLAUDIO

I know not how to pray your patience,
Yet I must speak. Choose your revenge yourself;

260   Impose me to what penance your invention
Can lay upon my sin; yet sinned I not
But in mistaking.

DON PEDRO   By my soul, nor I;
And yet, to satisfy this good old man,
I would bend under any heavy weight
That he'll enjoin me to.

LEONATO

I cannot bid you bid my daughter live,

That were impossible; but, I pray you both,
Possess the people in Messina here
How innocent she died; and if your love
Can labour aught in sad invention,   270
Hang her an epitaph upon her tomb
And sing it to her bones, sing it tonight.
Tomorrow morning come you to my house;
And since you could not be my son-in-law,
Be yet my nephew. My brother hath a daughter,
Almost the copy of my child that's dead,
And she alone is heir to both of us.
Give her the right you should have given her cousin,
And so dies my revenge.

CLAUDIO   O noble sir!
Your over-kindness doth wring tears from me.   280
I do embrace your offer, and dispose
For henceforth of poor Claudio.

LEONATO
Tomorrow then I will expect your coming;
Tonight I take my leave. This naughty man
Shall face to face be brought to Margaret,
Who I believe was packed in all this wrong,
Hired to it by your brother.

BORACHIO   No, by my soul, she was not,
Nor knew not what she did when she spoke to me,
But always hath been just and virtuous
In anything that I do know by her.   290

DOGBERRY Moreover, sir, which indeed is not under
white and black, this plaintiff here, the offender, did call
me ass; I beseech you, let it be remembered in his
punishment. And also, the watch heard them talk of one
Deformed; they say he wears a key in his ear and a lock
hanging by it, and borrows money in God's name, the
which he hath used so long and never paid, that now

men grow hard-hearted and will lend nothing for God's
sake. Pray you, examine him upon that point.

LEONATO

300   I thank thee for thy care and honest pains.

DOGBERRY Your worship speaks like a most thankful and
reverend youth, and I praise God for you.

LEONATO There's for thy pains.

DOGBERRY God save the foundation!

LEONATO Go, I discharge thee of thy prisoner, and I
thank thee.

DOGBERRY I leave an arrant knave with your worship;
which I beseech your worship to correct yourself, for the
example of others. God keep your worship! I wish your
310   worship well; God restore you to health! I humbly give
you leave to depart; and if a merry meeting may be
wished, God prohibit it! Come, neighbour.

                              Exeunt Dogberry and Verges

LEONATO

Until tomorrow morning, lords, farewell.

ANTONIO

Farewell, my lords; we look for you tomorrow.

DON PEDRO

We will not fail.

CLAUDIO   Tonight I'll mourn with Hero.

                              Exeunt Don Pedro and Claudio

LEONATO (*to the Watch*)

Bring you these fellows on. We'll talk with Margaret,
How her acquaintance grew with this lewd fellow.

                              Exeunt

V.2   *Enter Benedick and Margaret*

BENEDICK Pray thee, sweet Mistress Margaret, deserve

well at my hands by helping me to the speech of
Beatrice.

MARGARET Will you then write me a sonnet in praise of
my beauty?

BENEDICK In so high a style, Margaret, that no man living shall come over it; for, in most comely truth, thou
deservest it.

MARGARET To have no man come over me! Why, shall I
always keep below stairs?   10

BENEDICK Thy wit is as quick as the greyhound's mouth;
it catches.

MARGARET And yours as blunt as the fencer's foils, which
hit, but hurt not.

BENEDICK A most manly wit, Margaret; it will not hurt a
woman. And so, I pray thee, call Beatrice; I give thee
the bucklers.

MARGARET Give us the swords; we have bucklers of our
own.

BENEDICK If you use them, Margaret, you must put in   20
the pikes with a vice; and they are dangerous weapons
for maids.

MARGARET Well, I will call Beatrice to you, who I think
hath legs.   *Exit Margaret*

BENEDICK And therefore will come.

> (*Sings*) The God of love,
>   That sits above,
>   And knows me, and knows me,
>   How pitiful I deserve –

I mean in singing; but in loving, Leander the good   30
swimmer, Troilus the first employer of panders, and a
whole bookful of these quondam carpet-mongers,
whose names yet run smoothly in the even road of a
blank verse, why, they were never so truly turned over

and over as my poor self in love. Marry, I cannot show
it in rhyme, I have tried; I can find out no rhyme to
'lady' but 'baby' – an innocent rhyme; for 'scorn',
'horn' – a hard rhyme; for 'school', 'fool' – a babbling
rhyme; very ominous endings. No, I was not born under
40   a rhyming planet, nor I cannot woo in festival terms.
       Enter Beatrice
Sweet Beatrice, wouldst thou come when I called thee?
BEATRICE Yea, signor, and depart when you bid me.
BENEDICK O, stay but till then!
BEATRICE 'Then' is spoken; fare you well now. And yet,
    ere I go, let me go with that I came, which is, with know-
    ing what hath passed between you and Claudio.
BENEDICK Only foul words; and thereupon I will kiss thee.
BEATRICE Foul words is but foul wind, and foul wind is
    but foul breath, and foul breath is noisome; therefore I
50   will depart unkissed.
BENEDICK Thou hast frighted the word out of his right
    sense, so forcible is thy wit. But I must tell thee plainly,
    Claudio undergoes my challenge; and either I must
    shortly hear from him, or I will subscribe him a coward.
    And I pray thee now, tell me for which of my bad parts
    didst thou first fall in love with me?
BEATRICE For them all together; which maintained so
    politic a state of evil that they will not admit any good
    part to intermingle with them. But for which of my good
60   parts did you first suffer love for me?
BENEDICK Suffer love! A good epithet, I do suffer love
    indeed, for I love thee against my will.
BEATRICE In spite of your heart, I think; alas, poor
    heart! If you spite it for my sake, I will spite it for yours;
    for I will never love that which my friend hates.
BENEDICK Thou and I are too wise to woo peaceably.
BEATRICE It appears not in this confession; there's not

one wise man among twenty that will praise himself.

BENEDICK An old, an old instance, Beatrice, that lived in
the time of good neighbours. If a man do not erect in   70
this age his own tomb ere he dies, he shall live no longer
in monument than the bell rings and the widow weeps.

BEATRICE And how long is that, think you?

BENEDICK Question – why, an hour in clamour and a
quarter in rheum. Therefore is it most expedient for the
wise, if Don Worm, his conscience, find no impediment
to the contrary, to be the trumpet of his own virtues, as
I am to myself. So much for praising myself, who, I
myself will bear witness, is praiseworthy. And now tell
me, how doth your cousin?   80

BEATRICE Very ill.

BENEDICK And how do you?

BEATRICE Very ill too.

BENEDICK Serve God, love me, and mend. There will I
leave you too, for here comes one in haste.

Enter Ursula

URSULA Madam, you must come to your uncle. Yonder's
old coil at home; it is proved my Lady Hero hath been
falsely accused, the Prince and Claudio mightily abused,
and Don John is the author of all, who is fled and gone.
Will you come presently?   90

BEATRICE Will you go hear this news, signor?

BENEDICK I will live in thy heart, die in thy lap and be
buried in thy eyes; and moreover, I will go with thee to
thy uncle's.   *Exeunt*

Enter Claudio, Don Pedro, Balthasar, and three or   V.3
four with tapers, all wearing mourning

CLAUDIO Is this the monument of Leonato?

LORD It is, my lord.

CLAUDIO (*reading from a scroll*)

Epitaph

Done to death by slanderous tongues
    Was the Hero that here lies:
Death, in guerdon of her wrongs,
    Gives her fame which never dies.
So the life that died with shame
Lives in death with glorious fame.
    Hang thou there upon the tomb
      Praising her when I am dumb.
Now, music, sound, and sing your solemn hymn.

Song

BALTHASAR

Pardon, goddess of the night,
Those that slew thy virgin knight;
For the which, with songs of woe,
Round about her tomb they go.
Midnight, assist our moan,
Help us to sigh and groan,
    Heavily, heavily.
Graves yawn and yield your dead,
Till death be utterèd,
    Heavily, heavily.

CLAUDIO

Now, unto thy bones good night!
Yearly will I do this rite.

DON PEDRO

Good morrow, masters; put your torches out;
    The wolves have preyed, and look, the gentle day,
Before the wheels of Phoebus, round about
    Dapples the drowsy east with spots of grey.
Thanks to you all, and leave us: fare you well.

CLAUDIO

    Good morrow, masters: each his several way.

DON PEDRO

    Come, let us hence, and put on other weeds;   30
    And then to Leonato's we will go.

CLAUDIO

    And Hymen now with luckier issue speed's
    Than this for whom we rendered up this woe.

                                              Exeunt

    Enter Leonato, Antonio, Benedick, Beatrice, Margaret,   **V.4**
    Ursula, Friar Francis, and Hero

FRIAR

    Did I not tell you she was innocent?

LEONATO

    So are the Prince and Claudio, who accused her
    Upon the error that you heard debated;
    But Margaret was in some fault for this,
    Although against her will, as it appears
    In the true course of all the question.

ANTONIO

    Well, I am glad that all things sort so well.

BENEDICK

    And so am I, being else by faith enforced
    To call young Claudio to a reckoning for it.

LEONATO

    Well, daughter, and you gentlewomen all,   10
    Withdraw into a chamber by yourselves,
    And when I send for you, come hither masked.
    The Prince and Claudio promised by this hour
    To visit me. You know your office, brother;
    You must be father to your brother's daughter,
    And give her to young Claudio.   *Exeunt ladies*

ANTONIO

   Which I will do with confirmed countenance.

BENEDICK

   Friar, I must entreat your pains, I think.

FRIAR

   To do what, signor?

BENEDICK

20   To bind me, or undo me – one of them.

   Signor Leonato, truth it is, good signor,

   Your niece regards me with an eye of favour.

LEONATO

   That eye my daughter lent her; 'tis most true.

BENEDICK

   And I do with an eye of love requite her.

LEONATO

   The sight whereof I think you had from me,

   From Claudio, and the Prince; but what's your will?

BENEDICK

   Your answer, sir, is enigmatical;

   But, for my will, my will is your good will

   May stand with ours, this day to be conjoined

30   In the state of honourable marriage –

   In which, good Friar, I shall desire your help.

LEONATO

   My heart is with your liking.

FRIAR   And my help.

   Here comes the Prince and Claudio.

     Enter Don Pedro and Claudio, and two or three others

DON PEDRO

   Good morrow to this fair assembly.

LEONATO

   Good morrow, Prince; good morrow, Claudio;

   We here attend you. Are you yet determined

   Today to marry with my brother's daughter?

CLAUDIO

    I'll hold my mind, were she an Ethiope.

LEONATO

    Call her forth, brother; here's the Friar ready.

                                 Exit Antonio

DON PEDRO

    Good morrow, Benedick. Why, what's the matter,   40

    That you have such a February face,

    So full of frost, of storm and cloudiness?

CLAUDIO

    I think he thinks upon the savage bull.

    Tush, fear not, man, we'll tip thy horns with gold,

    And all Europa shall rejoice at thee,

    As once Europa did at lusty Jove,

    When he would play the noble beast in love.

BENEDICK

    Bull Jove, sir, had an amiable low;

    And some such strange bull leaped your father's cow,

    And got a calf in that same noble feat   50

    Much like to you, for you have just his bleat.

CLAUDIO

    For this I owe you: here comes other reckonings.

    Enter Antonio, with the ladies masked

    Which is the lady I must seize upon?

ANTONIO

    This same is she, and I do give you her.

CLAUDIO

    Why, then she's mine. Sweet, let me see your face.

ANTONIO

    No, that you shall not, till you take her hand

    Before this Friar and swear to marry her.

CLAUDIO

    Give me your hand; before this holy Friar,

    I am your husband, if you like of me.

HERO (*unmasking*)
60   And when I lived, I was your other wife;
    And when you loved, you were my other husband.

CLAUDIO
    Another Hero!

HERO   Nothing certainer;
    One Hero died defiled, but I do live,
    And surely as I live, I am a maid.

DON PEDRO
    The former Hero! Hero that is dead!

LEONATO
    She died, my lord, but whiles her slander lived.

FRIAR
    All this amazement can I qualify,
    When, after that the holy rites are ended,
    I'll tell you largely of fair Hero's death.
70   Meantime let wonder seem familiar,
    And to the chapel let us presently.

BENEDICK
    Soft and fair, Friar. Which is Beatrice?

BEATRICE (*unmasking*)
    I answer to that name. What is your will?

BENEDICK
    Do not you love me?

BEATRICE   Why no, no more than reason.

BENEDICK
    Why, then your uncle and the Prince and Claudio
    Have been deceived; they swore you did.

BEATRICE
    Do not you love me?

BENEDICK   Troth no, no more than reason.

BEATRICE
    Why, then my cousin, Margaret, and Ursula
    Are much deceived; for they did swear you did.

BENEDICK

They swore that you were almost sick for me.   80

BEATRICE

They swore that you were well-nigh dead for me.

BENEDICK

'Tis no such matter. Then you do not love me?

BEATRICE

No, truly, but in friendly recompense.

LEONATO

Come, cousin, I am sure you love the gentleman.

CLAUDIO

And I'll be sworn upon't that he loves her,
For here's a paper written in his hand,
A halting sonnet of his own pure brain,
Fashioned to Beatrice.

HERO   And here's another
Writ in my cousin's hand, stolen from her pocket,
Containing her affection unto Benedick.   90

BENEDICK A miracle! Here's our own hands against our
   hearts. Come, I will have thee; but, by this light, I take
   thee for pity.

BEATRICE I would not deny you; but, by this good day, I
   yield upon great persuasion; and partly to save your
   life, for I was told you were in a consumption.

BENEDICK (*kissing her*) Peace! I will stop your mouth.

DON PEDRO How dost thou, Benedick the married man?

BENEDICK I'll tell thee what, Prince; a college of wit-
   crackers cannot flout me out of my humour. Dost thou   100
   think I care for a satire or an epigram? No; if a man will
   be beaten with brains, 'a shall wear nothing handsome
   about him. In brief, since I do purpose to marry, I will
   think nothing to any purpose that the world can say
   against it; and therefore never flout at me for what I
   have said against it; for man is a giddy thing, and this

is my conclusion. For thy part, Claudio, I did think to
have beaten thee; but in that thou art like to be my kinsman, live unbruised and love my cousin.

CLAUDIO I had well hoped thou wouldst have denied
Beatrice, that I might have cudgelled thee out of thy
single life, to make thee a double-dealer; which out of
question thou wilt be, if my cousin do not look exceeding narrowly to thee.

BENEDICK Come, come, we are friends. Let's have a
dance ere we are married, that we may lighten our own
hearts and our wives' heels.

LEONATO We'll have dancing afterward.

BENEDICK First, of my word; therefore play, music.
Prince, thou art sad; get thee a wife, get thee a wife.
There is no staff more reverend than one tipped with
horn.

Enter a Messenger

MESSENGER
My lord, your brother John is ta'en in flight,
And brought with armed men back to Messina.

BENEDICK Think not on him till tomorrow; I'll devise
thee brave punishments for him. Strike up, pipers.

                    Dance, and then exeunt

An Account of the Text

Much Ado About Nothing was first published in 1600 in an edition believed to have been printed from a manuscript written by Shakespeare himself; this edition is known as the Quarto (Q). The play was then included in the collected edition of Shakespeare's plays published in 1623, and known as the Folio (F). Here it was printed, with some minor changes, from a copy of the Quarto. Many of these changes appear to have no authority, but some add information derived from the playhouse, and a few are of particular interest as reflecting a deliberate editing of the Quarto. At one point the Quarto adds a line of verse which seems to have been omitted accidentally from the Folio (I.1.288–9); elsewhere two passages were cut from the Folio text, apparently because of censorship (see the second list of collations, below). One passage (IV.2.17–20) plays too freely with the name of God, and may have been excised as a result of the Act to restrain abuses of players passed in 1606; the other reflects harshly on German and Spanish fashions, and is thought to have been cut when the play was revived in 1612–13 in connection with the marriage of Princess Elizabeth to the Elector Palatine.

The edition closest to Shakespeare's manuscript is the Quarto, on which the present edition is based. The Quarto contains relatively few errors, and these were corrected in the Folio or in subsequent editions (see collations 1 and 3). The Folio shows many minor differences, and sometimes makes equally good but different sense; in this edition the readings of the Quarto are preferred, as generally more authoritative, but since some Folio corrections or additions have authority, a list of the significant alterations not adopted in the present edition is given in the fourth list of collations.

The Quarto of *Much Ado About Nothing* has in common with other texts thought to have been printed from Shakespeare's manuscript a casual punctuation, and some disconcerting inconsistencies. The dramatist seems to have used the comma as his most usual mark of punctuation, and the Quarto text is lightly punctuated, with relatively few heavy stops, and far less pointing than the modern reader would expect. By contrast, the Folio of 1623, the texts for which were edited in the printing-house, has a very heavy punctuation, marked by frequent employment of the colon in a way now unfamiliar. The present edition is punctuated afresh according to modern usage, but as lightly as is compatible with the phrasing of the text. The few places where the punctuation offers real difficulty, as at II.1.41, are noted in the third list of collations.

In the stage directions and speech-prefixes of the Quarto there are many inconsistencies and inadequacies, such as might arise in an author's manuscript. These are in the main of three kinds. Firstly, the same character may be designated differently in different scenes, or even within a single scene. So Don Pedro appears in stage directions and speech-prefixes as both '(Don) Pedro' and 'Prince', Antonio often appears as 'Old' or 'Old man', or as Leonato's brother, and Dogberry and Verges are given their own names sometimes, at other times are called 'Const(able)' and 'Head(borough)', and in part of IV.2 the actors for whom Shakespeare wrote these parts are named in speech-prefixes as 'Ke(mp)' and 'Cowley'. Secondly, the stage directions are sometimes vague, or incomplete; occasionally more, at other times fewer, characters are named in an entry than have a part in a scene (as at II.1.192, where the Quarto has '*Enter the Prince, Hero, Leonato, Iohn, and Borachio, and Conrade*'; the three last-named characters have no part in the rest of this scene, and clearly must not be onstage); and many exits are not given at all. Thirdly, a notable ghost-character appears in the entries to I.1 and II.1, namely Leonato's wife ('Innogen'). She has no lines, and is not mentioned later in the play.

These confusions were at one time thought to be evidence of revision by Shakespeare, but this theory is discredited. The best explanation is that the Quarto is based on an author's manuscript in which he worked out the play as he went along, dropping 'Innogen' as an unnecessary part, and not troubling about consistency. The confusions in the Quarto would make it impracticable for use in the theatre, where a prompt copy must be consistent in names and directions. The Folio text makes some alterations which seem to stem from the theatre, including, notably, the substitution of the name '*Iacke Wilson*' for the direction '*Musicke*' in the Quarto at II.3.34. John Wilson is the name of a known musician of the time, who must have played Balthasar the singer before 1623. However, the Folio retains most of the confusions of the Quarto, and seems to have been modified by a few corrections from a prompt copy.

The text we have of the play is not then derived from the theatre. In the present edition stage directions have been made, amplified, cut or added to where necessary, and speech-prefixes have been made consistent. All this has been silently done, except where significant alterations have been necessary, or questions of disputed interpretation are involved; such cases (like the substitution of the speech-prefix BALTHASAR for *Bene* (*dick*) at II.1.88) are referred to the Commentary or in the collations. The 'long s' (ʃ) has been replaced by 's'.

COLLATIONS

1

The following is a list of readings in the present text of *Much Ado About Nothing* which differ from Q, and were first given in F. The reading of Q is printed on the right of the square bracket.

II.1
     76 *masquers, with a drum*] *not in* Q
II.3
     23 an] and
     137 us of] of vs
III.1
     0 *Ursula*] Vrsley
     4 Ursula] *Vrsley*

III.2

46 DON PEDRO] *Bene.*

III.4

17 in] it

V.3

10 dumb] dead

V.4

7 sort] sorts

2

The following is a list of passages in Q which were omitted from F, the second probably in the interests of political censorship (see above, p. 93), the fourth probably because it appeared blasphemous (see above, p. 93), and the others perhaps by oversight. They are printed as they appear in this edition.

I.1

288–9 and with her father | And thou shalt have her

III.2

31–4 or in the shape of two countries at once, as, a German from the waist downward, all slops, and a Spaniard from the hip upward, no doublet

IV.1

18 not knowing what they do

IV.2

17–20 CONRADE *and* BORACHIO Yea, sir, we hope.
DOGBERRY Write down, that they hope they serve God – and write God first, for God defend but God should go before such villains!

V.4

33 Here comes the Prince and Claudio.

3

The following readings in the present text of *Much Ado About Nothing* differ from those of both Q and F. Most of the alterations were first made in subsequent Folios (1632, 1664, 1685), or by eighteenth-century editors. Those of special interest are

discussed in the Commentary. The reading on the right of the
square bracket is common to Q and F unless otherwise indicated.

The Characters in the Play] *not in* Q, F
I.1
      0 *Messina, Hero] Messina, Innogen his wife, Hero*
   1, 9 Pedro] *Peter*
    39 bird-bolt] burbolt
    82 Benedick] Benedict
  189 Pedro] *Pedro, Iohn the Bastard*
I.2
    21 *Attendants cross the stage, led by Antonio's son, and accom-*
       panied by Balthasar the musician] not in Q, F
II.1
     0 *Antonio] his brother, his wife*
      Margaret, and Ursula] and a kinsman
    41 Peter for the heavens;] *Peter: for the heavens,*
    76 *Don John] or dumbe Iohn*
88, 91, 93 BALTHASAR] *Bene.*
   192 *Enter Don Pedro, with Leonato and Hero] Enter the Prince,*
    Hero, Leonato, Iohn, and Borachio, and Conrade Q; *Enter*
    the Prince F
II.3
     1 *Enter Boy] not in* Q, F
    34 *Claudio] Musicke* Q; *and Iacke Wilson* F
    40 hid-fox] kid-foxe
III.2
    26 can] cannot
  112 her, tomorrow] her to morrow
III.3
 37, 86 FIRST WATCHMAN] *Watch*
44, 48, 53, 65 SECOND WATCHMAN] *Watch*
 168–9 CONRADE Masters – | FIRST WATCHMAN Never speak]
    Conr. Masters, neuer speake
III.5
    9 off] of
IV.1
  154 silent been] bin silent
  200 Princes] Princesse

IV.2

    0 *Enter Dogberry, Verges, and the Sexton*] *Enter the*
       Constables, Borachio, and the Towne clearke
    1 DOGBERRY] *Keeper*
    2 VERGES] *Cowley*
    4 DOGBERRY] *Andrew*
    9 DOGBERRY] *Kemp*
  66–7 VERGES Let them be – in the hands. | CONRADE Off,
       coxcomb!] *Couley. (Sex.* F) Let them be in the hands
       of Coxcombe.

V.1

    16 sorry wag] sorrow, wagge
  114 like] likt

V.3

    0 *Balthasar*] *not in* Q, F
    3 CLAUDIO] *against line* 11 *in* Q, F
   12 BALTHASAR] *not in* Q, F

V.4

    0 *Beatrice*] *not in* Q, F
  54, 56 ANTONIO] *Leo.*
   97 BENEDICK] *Leon.*
  126 *FINIS*] *omitted in the present edition*

4

The following is a list of readings in the present text of *Much
Ado About Nothing* which stem from Q, but which were signifi-
cantly altered in F. So far as is known these alterations have no
authority, but some have been preferred by editors and still
appear in a variety of editions. Obvious errors and omissions are
not included here; the reading of F is printed on the right of the
square bracket.

I.1

    89 are you] you are
    99 doubt, sir] doubt
  138 That] This
  210 spoke] speake
  291 you do] doe you

I.2

  4 strange news] newes

I.3

  8 at least] yet
  22 true root] root
  36 make] will make

II.1

  49 say, 'Father, as] say, as
  70 sink] sinks
  86 Jove] Love
  197 I told] told
 200–201 him up a] him a
  223 that I was duller] and that I was duller
  252 my] this
  256 his] a
  271 that] a

II.2

  33 in love] in a love
  44 truth] truths

II.3

  31 not I for] not for
  40 *Enter Balthasar with music*] not in F
  70 fraud of men was] frauds of men were
  157 make but] but make
  205 unworthy so] unworthy to have so
 210–11 gentlewomen] gentlewoman
  218 their] the

III.1

  12 propose] purpose
  58 she'll] she
  104 limed] tame

III.2

  36 it appear] it to appear
 56–7 conclude, conclude] conclude
  117 midnight] night

III.3

  35 to talk] talk
  42 those] them
  77 statutes] Statues

135 and I see] and see
147 they] thy

III.4

42 see] looke

III.5

23 pound] times
46 as it may] as may
54 examination these] examine those

IV.1

20 ah, ha] ha, ha
74 do so] doe
85 are you] you are
94 spoke] spoken
131 smirchèd] smeered
150 the two Princes] the Princes
159 beat] bear
271 swear] sweare by it
287 deny it] denie
311 count, Count Comfect] Count, Confect
327 so I leave] so leave

IV.2

49 by mass] by th'masse
62-3 Leonato's] Leonato
80 any is in] any in

V.1

6 comforter] comfort

V.2

33 names] name
35-6 show it in] shew in
72 monument] monuments
bell rings] bels ring

V.4

33 *and two or three others*] *with attendants*
105 for what I] for I

Commentary

Biblical references are to the Bishops' Bible (1568, etc.), the official English translation of Elizabeth's reign. The abbreviations Q and F refer respectively to the Quarto and first Folio editions (see An Account of the Text, above).

The Title: *Much Ado About Nothing* exemplifies a kind of deliberately puzzling title that seems to have been popular in the late 1590s (cf. *As You Like It*, or the plays staged by the rival company to Shakespeare's, the Lord Admiral's Men, under titles like *Crack Me This Nut* and *Chance Medley*). The title *Much Ado About Nothing* has, of course, a direct meaning in relation to the play's main action, concerning Claudio and Hero, which proves in the end to be ado about nothing. It also contains a pun on the word 'noting', as illustrated by Don Pedro's remark on Balthasar at II.3.55: *Note, notes, forsooth, and nothing*; here the quibble is mainly on 'noting' as notation in a musical score. In the title, the sense 'observing' seems stronger, as the play is much concerned with people observing and overhearing one another, and making a great deal out of nothing. The implications have been fully worked out by P. A. Jorgensen in *Redeeming Shakespeare's Words* (1962).

I.1

o *Messina*: The setting is taken from Bandello. King Peter of Aragon, ruler of Sicily, held court in Messina after the Sicilian Vespers in 1283; he died in 1285. Both Q and F list *Innogen his wife* as entering after Leonato, but she has no part in the play.

   0 *Hero*: She embodies faithfulness in love, as her name recalls the story of Hero and Leander; see also IV.1.80 and note, and V.2.30–31.

1, 9 *Pedro*: Q and F have *Peter* here; for other anglicizations of names, see III.1.0 and 4, and V.1.91 (Antony).

   6 *action*: Battle.

   7 *name*: Distinction.

12–13 *equally remembered*: Justly rewarded.

13–16 *He hath borne himself . . . tell you how*: The Messenger's manner is slightly pompous; his speech combines antithesis and alliteration, with an echo of euphuism.

  17 *uncle*: The uncle does not appear in the play.

  21 *modest*: Moderate.

21–2 *badge of bitterness*: Tears. Their master's 'badge' or device was worn by servants on the sleeve, a mark of humble status, and so of modesty.

  25 *kind*: Natural.

  28 *Mountanto*: Upright thrust in fencing. Beatrice well knows Benedick as a (verbal) duellist with her.

  31 *sort*: Rank.

  34 *pleasant*: Merry.

  36 *set up his bills*: Posted notices.

  37 *at the flight*: To a shooting contest. Benedick claims to be a better archer than Cupid, that is, a ladykiller, and, as he says later, a *tyrant to their sex* (158–9). See Introduction, p. xxiv.

  38 *subscribed for*: Signed on behalf of.

  39 *bird-bolt*: Blunt-headed arrow used for shooting birds; it was also the allowed weapon of the fool (cf. the proverb 'a fool's bolt is soon shot'), as being fairly harmless. Benedick claimed expert skill in challenging Cupid; the fool implies that he is a novice by challenging him at the lowest level of archery.

  42 *tax*: Disparage.

  43 *meet*: Even.

  46 *holp*: The early strong inflection only gradually gave way to the modern 'helped'; Shakespeare uses both forms.

  47 *valiant trencher-man*: Hearty eater.

50 *to*: In comparison with.

52 *stuffed*: Well-stored (a proper usage).

54 *stuffed man*: Suggesting a figure stuffed to look like a
    man.

61 *five wits*: Mental faculties, numbered five by vague
    analogy with the five senses, and sometimes named as
    common sense, imagination, fantasy, estimation and
    memory.
    halting: Limping.

63–4 *bear it for a difference*: In heraldry, to show 'an alter-
    ation of or an addition to a coat of arms, to distinguish
    a junior member or branch of a family from the chief
    line' (*Oxford English Dictionary*).

65–6 *reasonable creature*: This was a phrase applied to all
    living creatures, not just to human beings; Beatrice
    implies that Benedick is little better than his horse.

69 *faith*: Loyalty to his *sworn brother*.

71 *block*: Mould (and so shape or fashion).

72 *books*: Good books, favour.

73, 178, 187 *an*: If.

75 *squarer*: Swaggerer.

81 *presently*: At once.

84 *I will hold friends with you*: I will take care not to cross
    you.

86 *run mad*: Catch the Benedick, and meaning also 'fall in
    love with him'.

88 *is*: Has (a survival of an old usage with verbs of motion).
    the Bastard: The first indication in the text that Don
    John is a bastard comes at IV.1.186. His bastardy partly
    explains his temperament; Bacon says in his essay *Of
    Envy* (1625): 'Bastards are envious: for he that cannot
    possibly mend his own case, will do what he can to
    impair others.'

90 *trouble*: The burden and expense of entertaining the
    Prince and his retinue.

96 *charge*: Expense, and responsibility.

101 *have it full*: Are well answered.

102–3 *fathers herself*: Shows who her father is by resembling
    him.

106 *his head*: Meaning his beard and grey or white hair.

113 *meet*: Proper (with a quibble on 'meat').

114 *convert*: Change.

120 *dear happiness*: Precious piece of luck.

122 *of your humour for that*: Of your frame of mind on that point.

130 *rare parrot-teacher*: Fine chatterer. Like one teaching a parrot, she repeats herself and talks little sense, says Benedick.

131–2 *A bird of my tongue is better than a beast of yours*: A talking bird is better than a dumb beast.

134 *continuer*: One having the power to keep going.

136 *with a jade's trick*: By stopping suddenly, like an ill-tempered horse, and throwing me off.

138 *That is the sum of all, Leonato*: Don Pedro has been talking aside with Leonato, and now turns to include the others in his address.

140 *all*: Including Don John and Balthasar.

146 *being*: Since you are.

150 *Please it*: May it please.

154 *noted her not*: Did not give her special attention.

161 *low*: Short.

171 *sad*: Serious.

flouting Jack: Mocking knave. *Jack* was used as a common noun, meaning 'fellow'; cf. 'a swearing Jack', *The Taming of the Shrew*, II.1.281.

172–3 *Cupid is a good hare-finder . . . carpenter*: The joke is that Cupid was blind, and good sight is needed to spot a hare; and Vulcan, god of fire, was a blacksmith.

173 *go*: Join.

185 *wear his cap with suspicion*: Get married, and be suspected of wearing a cap to hide his cuckold's horns.

188 *sigh away Sundays*: Because on Sundays, or days of leisure, he will feel his bondage most sharply.

197 *who*: Whom (a common usage).

part: That is, to ask that question.

199 *If this were so, so were it uttered*: Claudio speaks evasively: 'If I had told him such a secret, he would have revealed it in this way.'

200 *old tale*: An old tale which contains the refrain quoted
    was reported in the 1821 Variorum edition of Shake-
    speare; its authenticity is doubtful, but it illustrates
    Benedick's meaning. In it a villain repeatedly denies
    his crimes when they are described to him, until at last
    proof is laid before him; so, however much Claudio
    denies that he is in love, the truth is evident.

206 *fetch me in*: Trick me into a confession.

209 *two faiths and troths*: Joking allusion to the clash
    between his loyalty to Don Pedro and his friendship
    to Claudio.

216–17 *in the despite of*: In showing contempt for.

218–19 *in the force of his will*: By mere obstinacy (suggesting
    the wilfulness of the heretic in maintaining a false
    opinion).

222–3 *have a recheat . . . invisible baldrick*: Have a call for
    assembling the hounds sounded in my forehead, or hang
    my hunting-horn in an invisible belt. In other words,
    Benedick will be neither an open nor an unacknowl-
    edged cuckold, will neither display nor conceal
    cuckold's horns – implying that one or other is the fate
    of all married men.

226 *fine*: Conclusion.

230–31 *lose more blood with love . . . drinking*: It was commonly
    believed that sighing dried up the blood and that
    drinking wine produced new blood.

232 *ballad-maker's*: As ballads were mainly of love.

236 *argument*: Topic for conversation.

237 *hang me in a bottle like a cat*: A cat suspended in a
    leather bottle or basket was used sometimes as a target
    for practice in archery.

239 *Adam*: After Adam Bell, a famous archer.

241 *'In time the savage bull doth bear the yoke'*: The line is
    roughly quoted from Thomas Kyd's *The Spanish
    Tragedy* (*c.* 1587), II.1.3: 'In time the savage bull sustains
    the yoke', where, in turn, it is borrowed from Sonnet
    47 of Thomas Watson's *Hecatompathia* (1582).

249 *horn-mad*: Furious (as bulls attack with horns when
    enraged – and with an allusion also to cuckolds' horns).

251 *Venice*: In Shakespeare's day, a city famous for its cour-
tesans and sexual licence.

252 *earthquake*: Meaning that it will take a huge convulsion
to affect him.

253 *temporize with the hours*: Weaken as time goes by.

258 *matter*: Sense.

260 *tuition*: Care. Claudio parodies the formal ending of a
letter.

265 *guarded*: Ornamented.

266 *basted*: Loosely tacked on.

266–7 *flout old ends*: Mock me with old tags (like the
quotation at 241 and the parody at 260–63). *old ends*
suggest also the *fragments* of cloth of the previous
sentence.

269 *do me good*: Help me.

275 *affect*: Care for.

276 *ended action*: War just ended.

280 *now I*: Now that I.

283 *prompting*: Reminding.

286 *book of words*: As every lover should pour out words,
preferably rhymes, in praise of his mistress. Even
Benedick tries his hand at it in V.2.

288 *break*: Broach the matter.

292 *complexion*: Appearance (the lover looks pale).

294 *salved it*: Accounted for it (a sense once common).
treatise: Narrative.

296 *The fairest grant is the necessity*: The best gift is what
satisfies a need.

297 *Look what*: Whatever.
'Tis once: Once for all.

302 *in her bosom*: Privately to her.
unclasp: As if it were a book with the covers fastened
between clasps.

I.2

0 *his brother*: The name of Leonato's brother is not given
here in Q or F, and is only established in the dialogue
at V.1.100.

1 *cousin*: Used generally to mean 'kinsman'; Antonio's
son is not mentioned again after this scene.

5 *they*: The news, or new tidings, properly a plural.

6 *event*: Outcome.

8 *thick-pleached*: Thickly hedged with intertwined branches.

10 *discovered*: Revealed.

12 *accordant*: Sympathetic.

13 *take the present time by the top*: Seize the opportunity
   (an allusion to the proverb 'take Occasion by the fore-
   lock, for she is bald behind').

15 *wit*: Intelligence.

22–4 *Cousin . . . cousin*: Antonio's son, who leads on the
   attendants and the musician.

23 *cry you mercy*: Beg your pardon.

I.3

1 *What the good-year*: A general expletive, equivalent to
   'What the devil!'.

2 *out of measure*: Excessively.

9 *sufferance*: Endurance.

11 *born under Saturn*: And ruled by its astrological influence, making him gloomy and 'saturnine'.

12 *mortifying mischief*: Killing misfortune. He is thinking
   of his defeat in battle, his being taken prisoner and his
   bastardy.

16 *claw*: Flatter (literally, scratch; cf. the modern 'scratch
   one's back').

25 *canker*: Dog-rose. Don John would rather be inde-
   pendent, like the wild rose in the hedge, than nurtured
   under his brother's influence. Cf. Shakespeare's Sonnet
   54 for a similar contrast.

26 *blood*: Disposition, and family status as a bastard of the
   blood royal.

27 *carriage*: Mode of behaviour.

30 *trusted with a muzzle*: Don John likens himself to a
   beast, muzzled and hobbled, not trusted and not really
   free; his complaint is unjustified but the image perhaps
   appropriate.

31 *clog*: Block attached to the head or leg of an animal,
   preventing it from escaping.

36 *use it only*: Do nothing else but cultivate it.

37 *Borachio*: '*Borracho*' is Spanish for 'drunkard'. Borachio

lives up to his name, as is seen at III.3.102.

42 *model*: Design; originally, an architect's drawings for a projected building.

43 *What is he for a fool*: What sort of a fool is he?

48 *proper squire*: Fine young lover. Don John pours his scorn on Claudio.

52 *March-chick*: Precocious youngster (like a bird hatched very early in spring).

54 *entertained for*: Hired as.

55 *smoking*: Perfuming or fumigating. So Leonato's house was prepared for guests.

56 *sad*: Serious.

57 *arras*: Tapestries hung on the walls of rooms for warmth and decoration, often mounted far enough away from the wall to allow a man to hide in the space between.

61 *start-up*: Upstart.

62 *cross*: Thwart, but quibbling on the meaning 'make the sign of the cross', so leading to 'bless' (benefit).

63 *sure*: Reliable.

67–8 *Would the cook were o'my mind*: Don John fantasizes about poisoning the happy group at supper.

68 *prove*: Find out by experience.

II.1

The supper spoken of in I.3 is now over and dancing is about to begin.

9 *my lady's eldest son*: A widow's eldest son, and so a spoiled child and a foolish talker.

17 *shrewd*: Sharp.

18 *curst*: Ill-tempered.

20–21 *'God sends a curst cow short horns'*: This is proverbial and means 'God takes care that the vicious lack power to do harm'.

24 *Just*: Just so.
   husband: Beatrice makes the common play on *horns* as both phallus and emblem of cuckoldry; see 38.

27 *lie in the woollen*: Sleep between rough blankets (instead of sheets).

34–5 *take sixpence . . . lead his apes into hell*: The proverbial fate of a woman who died an old maid was to lead apes

in hell. The *bear-ward*, or bear-keeper, was a familiar
figure in Shakespeare's London, where bear-baiting, in
which mastiff dogs were set to attack a chained bear,
was a favourite sport.

41 *Saint Peter*: As gatekeeper of heaven; see Matthew
16:19.

for the heavens: A common interjection, especially
appropriate here as she is thinking of heaven.

42 *bachelors*: Unmarried men and women.

52 *metal*: Material (but also 'mettle' or spirit, earth being
dull and heavy).

53–5 *earth . . . clod of wayward marl*: This alludes to Genesis
2:7: 'God also did shape man, even of the dust of the
ground'; Beatrice's jest is that woman was made of
Adam's rib and not of earth.

56–7 *brethren . . . kindred*: Reference to the 'Table of Kindred
and Affinity' included in the *Book of Common Prayer*
and listing the relatives a man and woman may not
marry.

59 *in that kind*: In that way (that is, concerning marriage).

62 *in good time*: Quibbling on *time* as measure or tempo
in music.

62–3 *important*: Pressing.

63 *measure*: Moderation (but also a kind of stately dance).

66 *cinquepace*: Lively dance (French '*cinq pas*' = five paces).
The word was pronounced 'sink a pace' – hence the
pun at 70.

68 *ancientry*: Old-fashioned formality.

69 *bad legs*: Presumably a mark of decrepitude.

72 *passing*: Very.

77 *walk a bout*: As couples pair off for the dance.

friend: Lover.

84 *favour*: Looks.

84–5 *God defend . . . the case*: God forbid that your face
should be like your mask.

86 *Philemon's roof; within the house is Jove*: Philemon, a
peasant, entertained Jupiter hospitably in his humble
cottage, which, in the account of the legend Shakespeare
knew, in Arthur Golding's translation of Ovid,

Metamorphoses, 8.806, was 'thatched all with straw'.
Lines 86–7 form 'fourteeners', rhymed verses with
seven accents, the measure of Golding's Ovid.

87 *visor*: Mask.

88, 91, 93 *Balthasar*: In Q and F these lines are assigned to
Benedick, but the pairs of dancers talk in turn and
Benedick is paired with Beatrice at 111, so that there is
good reason to think the speeches wrongly assigned
here.

98 *clerk*: Parish clerk, who led the responses in church
services.

101 *At a word*: Briefly.

102 *waggling*: Trembling of old age.

105 *dry*: Dried or withered.
up and down: All over.

116 *'Hundred Merry Tales'*: A common jest-book, first
printed in 1525.

124 *only his*: His only.
impossible: Incredible.

126 *villainy*: Coarseness.

126–7 *pleases men and angers them*: Pleases by being rude about
others, and angers by slandering his hearers.

128 *fleet*: Company (the *fleet* of couples sailing in the dance).
boarded: The word plays on two meanings, the first
metaphorical, taking up the *fleet* metaphor (as in
boarding a ship), and the second meaning 'to accost or
woo'. See Introduction, pp. xxxi–xxxii.

135 *partridge wing*: This has almost no meat on it; her jest
is to suggest that Benedick's appetite is at best minimal.

137 *leaders*: The first couple in the dance.

156 *banquet*: Dessert of sweetmeats, fruit and wine, served
separately as a refreshment after the dance.

161 *office*: Business.

165 *faith*: A friend's loyalty.
blood: Passion.

166 *accident of hourly proof*: Common happening (one seen
every hour).

172 *willow*: The common emblem of unrequited love.

173 *County*: Count (a common form).

174 *usurer's chain*: The fashion was for wealthy men to wear
    a gold chain hanging on the breast.

175 *scarf*: Sash worn by soldiers diagonally across the body
    from one shoulder. Benedick implies that Claudio will
    either make money out of the loss of Hero by
    demanding something of the Prince, or else will chal-
    lenge the Prince to a fight.

178 *drovier*: Drover, cattle-dealer.

182–3 *strike like the blind man . . . beat the post*: That is, strike
    out wildly. The allusion is to Lazarillo de Tormes, the
    boy-hero of a Spanish romance, who leads a blind
    master about. An English translation was published in
    1586.

184 *If it will not be*: If you will not leave me.

190–91 *puts the world into her person*: Assumes that the world's
    opinion of me is the same as her own personal opinion.

191 *gives me out*: Reports me.

192.1 *Enter Don Pedro, with Leonato and Hero*: Q adds Don
    John, Borachio and Conrade for good measure, but this
    must be an error. Most editors adopt the F arrange-
    ment, and only bring on Don Pedro here, with Leonato
    and Hero entering at 239; but Hero must be onstage
    at 198 (*this young lady*), and it is appropriate for her to
    enter with her father, not with Claudio.

195–6 *part of Lady Fame*: In spreading rumour.

196–7 *lodge in a warren*: A gamekeeper's lodge in a park,
    which would be lonely, and so breed melancholy.

212 *them*: The young birds in the nest.

214–15 *If their singing answer your saying . . . honestly*: If what
    you say proves true, then indeed you speak honourably.

219 *misused*: Abused.

223–4 *duller than a great thaw*: For then roads were impass-
    able, and people were forced to stay at home.

225 *impossible conveyance*: Incredible skill.

226 *mark*: Target.

228 *terminations*: The sharp endings of her sentences.

232–3 *Hercules have turned spit . . . make the fire too*: This
    alludes to the legend of Omphale, Queen of Lydia,
    who made Hercules her slave, dressed him as a woman

and set him to spin. To turn the spit was an even more menial task.

234 *Ate*: Goddess of discord.

235 *scholar*: One who knew Latin, the language of exorcism. *conjure her*: Expel the evil spirits out of her.

235–7 *while she is here ... as in a sanctuary*: Hell itself becomes a place of refuge while she is on earth.

244 *tooth-picker*: Fashionable toothpicks were made of precious materials like gold and silver and often jewelled, hence the need to go to Asia for them.

245 *Prester John*: Legendary king, supposed to rule a Christian country in a remote part of Asia or Africa.

246 *great Cham*: Emperor of China.

247 *Pigmies*: Legendary race of dwarfs, supposed to live beyond India, or in Ethiopia. The existence of real dwarf races in Africa was not known in Europe until the nineteenth century.

255–8 *lent it me awhile ... I have lost it*: This passage refers to a previous love-affair between Beatrice and Benedick, not shown in the play but suggesting a long-established familiarity between them. Beatrice juggles with meanings; the interest (*use*) she gave was her own heart (double his single one), but a false one (*double* meaning also *deceitful*). Thus she repays him with deceit for an occasion when he deceived her with *false dice* into thinking she loved him.

270 *civil as an orange*: Punning on 'Seville'; Claudio is bitter-sweet, like a Seville orange.

271 *jealous complexion*: Yellow was the traditional colour of jealousy, perhaps because the melancholy humour (one of the four humours on which contemporary medical theory was based) was associated with jaundice.

272 *blazon*: Description.

273 *conceit*: Conception (of what has happened).

275 *broke with*: Told.

279–80 *all Grace*: God, the fountainhead of grace.

289 *poor fool*: Poor dear (an expression of tenderness).

290 *windy side*: Away from, as a sailing-ship kept to windward to avoid attack.

292–3 *cousin . . . for alliance*: Claudio claims his new rela-
       tionship by marriage (or *alliance*) in calling Beatrice
       cousin, and she picks this up in her retort.

293–4 *goes every one to the world*: Everyone gets married.

294   *sunburnt*: Dried up and ugly to Elizabethans – who
       prized a white skin in a woman – and hence, neglected.

295   *'Heigh-ho for a husband!'*: Title of an old ballad.

297   *getting*: Begetting (as Beatrice chooses to interpret the
       word).

310   *star danced*: So influencing her temperament; see I.3.11
       and note.

314   *cry you mercy*: Beg your pardon.

314–15 *By your grace's pardon*: Please excuse me.

318   *sad*: Serious.

319   *ever*: Always.

320   *unhappiness*: Misfortune.

323–4 *out of suit*: Out of wooing her (see 66).

333   *a just seven-night*: An exact week.

334   *answer my mind*: As I would like to have them.

336   *breathing*: Delay.

344   *watchings*: Loss of sleep, as we would now say.

347   *modest*: Consistent with modesty.

351   *strain*: Lineage.
       approved: Tested.

II.2

1   *shall*: Is going to.

3   *cross*: Thwart.

6–7   *whatsoever comes athwart . . . with mine*: Whatever foils
       his desire goes along with (and so satisfies) mine.

8   *covertly*: Secretly.

19   *temper*: Concoct.

22   *estimation*: Worth.

23   *stale*: Prostitute.

25   *misuse*: Deceive.
       vex: Torment. Its meaning was stronger than in modern
       usage.

30   *meet hour*: Suitable time.

32   *intend*: Pretend.

35   *cozened*: Cheated.

37 *trial*: Evidence.

38 *instances*: Examples.

39–40 *hear me call Margaret Hero . . . Claudio*: Margaret is to
be persuaded to impersonate Hero, while Borachio
pretends to be Claudio. Thus she will not suspect
villainy, and the Prince and Claudio will think that Hero
is mocking Claudio as well as deceiving him, by play-
acting with another lover under his name. Margaret is
presented as loyal and virtuous in Act V, and nowhere
appears in Act IV, where she might have saved Hero
by revealing all. No one notices this on the stage,
however, and the difficulties which have caused some
editors to emend *Claudio* here to *Borachio* appear only
in reading the play.

44–5 *jealousy shall be called assurance*: Suspicion shall be
called certainty.

45 *preparation*: For the wedding.

51 *presently*: At once.

II.3

5–7 *I am here already . . . again*: The Boy means 'it is as
good as done', but Benedick jokes by taking his words
literally.

11 *argument*: Subject.

14 *drum and the fife*: Associated with military music. The
fife was a shrill flute-like instrument.

14–15 *tabor and the pipe*: Small drum and reed instrument,
associated with festivals and social gatherings.

17 *carving*: Designing.

19–20 *turned orthography*: Become pedantic in his language.
Shakespeare meant that he had become a rhetorician
or euphuist (see I.1.13–16 and note), concerned for
flowers of style.

25–7 *fair . . . wise . . . virtuous*: These are just the adjectives
he applies to Beatrice later on; see 224–6 below.

30 *cheapen*: Make a bid for.

31 *noble, or not I for an angel*: Punning on the names of
coins. These were originally names for the same coin
but in Shakespeare's day the angel was worth 10s., and
the noble 6s. 8d.

34 *arbour*: A property 'arbour', seemingly made of a wooden trellis, and covered with what look like leaves, is shown on the title page of Kyd's *The Spanish Tragedy* (printed 1592).

Enter Don Pedro, Leonato, and Claudio: Q calls for *Musicke* here, anticipating the entry of Balthasar at 40. F omits the entry for Balthasar at 40, and, in place of *Musicke* here, has *and Iacke Wilson*, that is, John Wilson, the name of a musician in Shakespeare's company who played the part of Balthasar.

40 *We'll fit the hid-fox with a pennyworth*: That is, we'll pay him out for his craftiness in hiding. Q and F have *kid-fox*, which makes no sense, and 'k' for 'h' is a simple mistake.

42 *tax not*: Do not order.

44 *the witness still*: Always evidence.

45 *put a strange face on*: Pretend not to know.

53 *noting*: Attending to, and setting down in a musical score.

54 *crotchets*: Both 'musical notes', and 'strange fancies'.

55 *Note notes, forsooth, and nothing*: Pay attention to your music and nothing else. *nothing* was pronounced like 'noting', and Don Pedro is playing on Balthasar's words in 53.

57 *sheep's guts*: The music is provided by a stringed instrument, probably a lute.

58 *horn*: As sounding to war, or to the hunt. Benedick, as a soldier, affects to despise music.

59 *The Song*: This, with the music, softens the mood, and prepares for talk of love. A setting for this song by a contemporary of Shakespeare, Thomas Ford, survives in manuscript; see F. W. Sternfeld, *Music in Shakespearean Tragedy* (1963), pp. 106–7. It is set for two tenors and a bass, so would not be suitable for performance in the play.

68 *moe*: More.

69 *dumps*: Sad songs.

79 *for a shift*: As a makeshift; for want of someone better.

80, 159 *An*: If.

83 *night-raven*: Whose cry was thought to portend death or sickness.

94 *stalk on*: Alluding to a stalking-horse, a tame beast made to walk slowly near to wildfowl, concealing the approach of the hunter, who kept behind it.

99–100 *Sits the wind in that corner*: Is that how things stand?

102 *enraged*: Passionate.

103 *it is past the infinite of thought*: In other words, no amount of thinking can alter that fact.

108 *discovers*: Reveals.

112 *sit you*: Ethical dative, equivalent to 'sit – note this!'. Invention fails Leonato here, and he hands over to Claudio.

120 *gull*: Trick.

121 *white-bearded*: Marking Leonato's old age; see V.1.50.

124 *hold it up*: Keep the fiction going.

134 *smock*: Chemise. Women commonly slept in their undergarments, or smocks, and the word 'nightgown' meant 'dressing-gown'; see III.4.17 and note.

140–41 *sheet? That*: In Q and F *sheete. That* but the question mark makes the sense clear; Leonato asks 'do you mean this particular one?', in effect, and Claudio replies 'that's the one'. There is a quibble here, of course, on bed-sheets.

142–3 *halfpence*: Tiny pieces. The halfpenny was then a very small silver coin.

152 *ecstasy*: Frenzy.

156 *discover*: Reveal (see 108).

159 *alms*: Deed of charity.

164 *blood*: Passion.

167 *guardian*: Implying that Beatrice is an orphan.

168 *dotage*: Doting love.

169 *daffed all other respects*: Put aside all other considerations (such as the difference of rank).

176 *bate*: Abate, yield.

178 *tender*: Offer.

180 *contemptible*: Scornful.

181 *proper*: Handsome.

182 *good outward happiness*: Handsome appearance.

185 *wit*: Intelligence.

195 *large*: Coarse.

199 *counsel*: Resolution.

206 *Dinner*: The midday meal for Elizabethans, and not appropriate to the time, which is evening (36). There are many such trivial inconsistencies in Shakespeare's plays.

207 *upon*: As a result of.

211 *carry*: Manage.

212 *no such matter*: There is nothing of the sort.

214 *dumb-show*: Because they will be tongue-tied, and their usual banter will fail them.

216 *sadly borne*: Seriously conducted.

218 *have their full bent*: Are stretched to the limit (like a bow).

224–6 *fair . . . wise*: See 25–7 and note above.

226 *reprove*: Disprove.

229 *quirks*: Quips.

233 *sentences*: Epigrams (Latin *sententiae*).

234 *career*: Course (but see V.1.133 and note).

241 *Fair Beatrice, I thank you for your pains*: In the first flush of love, Benedick breaks into blank verse.

247 *daw*: Fool (properly, jackdaw).

248 *stomach*: Appetite, either for dinner or for repartee. Benedick is struck dumb (see 214).

250 *double meaning*: Benedick's interpretations are, of course, fanciful.

254 *Jew*: That is, no Christian. Charity, he thinks, demands that he love her.

III.1

0 *Ursula*: The spelling *Ursley* in Q here and at 4 indicates Hero's familiar pronunciation of the name.

3 *Proposing*: Conversing.

7 *pleachèd*: Formed by intertwined branches (see I.2.8). The comic irony is happier if this *bower* is represented by the same *arbour* that Benedick hid in.

9–11 *like favourites . . . bred it*: This is probably a general simile, but some think it was added in topical reference to the rebellion of the Earl of Essex in 1601.

12 *listen our propose*: Hear our conversation.
office: Task.

14 *presently*: At once.

16 *trace*: Tread.

24–5 *lapwing . . . by the ground*: The lapwing, or plover, draws intruders away from its nest in this fashion.

30 *woodbine coverture*: Honeysuckle shelter.

35 *coy*: Contemptuous.

36 *haggards*: Wild hawks.

45–6 *as full as . . . ever Beatrice shall couch upon*: In other words, a wife every bit as good as Beatrice.

52 *Misprizing*: Despising.

54 *All matter else seems weak*: All other discourse seems of little worth.

55 *project*: Conception.

56 *self-endeared*: In love with herself.

60 *How*: However.

61 *spell him backward*: Misrepresent him (line 68 is another way of saying it).

63 *black*: Swarthy.
     an antic: A grotesque figure.

65 *agate very vilely cut*: The allusion is to the tiny human figures often cut in agate stones used as seals.

70 *simpleness*: Integrity.
     purchaseth: Deserve. The two nouns form one concept, hence the verb is singular.

72 *from*: Contrary to.

76 *press me to death*: This alludes to '*peine forte et dure*', a punishment inflicted on criminals who refused to enter a plea; heavy weights were placed on the victim's chest until he pleaded or died.

79, 80 *with*: By.

84 *honest*: Innocent, and such as would not damage her reputation.

90 *prized*: Esteemed.

96 *argument*: Power to reason.

100 *married*: To be married.

101 *every day, tomorrow*: Every day in the sense that I shall be married for life, but the ceremony is tomorrow.

102 *attires*: Head-dresses.

103 *furnish*: Adorn.

104 *limed*: Snared (as with bird-lime).

105 *haps*: Chance.

107 *What fire is in mine ears*: This is an allusion to the common notion that a person's ears burn when others talk of him behind his back; the thought is continued in 110. In love, Beatrice, like Benedick (see II.3.241), bursts into verse, indeed into rhyming quatrains.

112 *Taming my wild heart*: She picks up the hawk image of 35–6 above.

116 *reportingly*: Merely by hearsay.

III.2

1–2 *consummate*: Consummated (once a proper form of the past participle).

3–4 *vouchsafe*: Allow.

7–8 *only be bold with Benedick*: Ask Benedick alone.

10 *hangman*: Used playfully to mean 'rascal'.

15 *sadder*: More serious.

17 *Hang him, truant*: Hang him for a rogue!

21–3 *Draw it . . . draw it afterwards*: The tooth. But *draw* also means disembowel, as convicted traitors were hanged, drawn and quartered, and Claudio takes the word up in this sense.

25 *Where*: Where there.
a humour or a worm: Supposed causes of decay in teeth. In the physiology of the day, humours were body fluids, and the thought here is of a morbid secretion of one of them.

26 *grief*: Pain.

29 *fancy*: Love.

30 *disguises*: Fashionable Englishmen were noted for their extravagance and constant change of fashion in clothes; see *The Merchant of Venice*, I.2.69–71.

33 *slops*: Loose breeches.

35 *he is no fool for fancy*: He is not making a fool of himself for love (though he may be doing so in affecting strange clothes).

42–3 *old ornament of his cheek . . . tennis-balls*: Beatrice cannot endure a bearded husband; see II.1.26–7.

46 *civet*: Perfume much used by gentlemen of the period.

52 *paint himself*: Use cosmetics.

55 *lute-string . . . governed by stops*: Benedick has turned lover, as love-songs were sung to the lute, a stringed instrument regulated by its *stops*, formerly rings of gut, now more commonly bars of wood or metal placed on the fingerboard.

61 *ill conditions*: Bad qualities.

62 *dies*: Fades away, and *dies* in the act of sex. See V.2.92–3 and note.

63 *buried with her face upwards*: Continuing the play on the act of sex; she will be smothered by Benedick.

66 *hobby-horses*: Buffoons. Originally a figure of a horse fastened round the waist of a morris-dancer.

68 *break with*: Speak to.

73 *e'en*: Evening: See V.1.46.

83 *discover*: Reveal.

86 *aim better at me*: Judge me better.
   that: That which.

87 *holds you well*: Loves you.

88 *dearness of heart*: Affection.

91–2 *circumstances shortened*: Omitting the details.

98 *paint out*: Display.

100–101 *warrant*: Proof.

117 *bear it coldly*: Keep calm about it.

119 *untowardly turned*: Wretchedly transformed.

III.3

0 *Dogberry*: Name for the fruit of the dogwood, mountain ash, dog-rose and various other plants; a general sense of rotundity and of redness seems warranted.
   compartner: Associate.
   Verges: The name represents a possible spelling of 'verjuice', the acid juice pressed out of unripe fruit, and hence a general term for 'sourness'. Perhaps these meanings give a clue to Shakespeare's idea of Dogberry and Verges; the former seems to have been large, and the latter old and thin or small, from the dialogue at III.5.32–9.
   the Watch: This consisted of those men chosen to act as policemen for the night.

3 *salvation*: Dogberry and Verges are always blundering
   into the opposite of what they mean.

7 *give them their charge*: Explain their duties to them.

9 *desartless*: Lacking in merit. Dogberry intends to say
   'deserving'.

10 *constable*: Deputy to Dogberry, who is the constable or
   officer responsible for supervising the maintenance of
   public order in a town or district.

14 *well-favoured*: Good-looking.

25 *vagrom*: Vagrant.
   stand: Halt.

37 *FIRST WATCHMAN*: From here to 122, neither Q nor F
   distinguishes in speech-prefixes between the two
   Watchmen, and the identifying of them as 'First' and
   'Second' is a pretty arbitrary matter.

38 *belongs to*: Is the task of.

39 *ancient*: Experienced.

41 *bills*: Halberds (weapons like a combined spear and
   battleaxe, which were used by infantry and by watchmen).

50 *true*: Honest.

51 *make*: Have to do.

56 *they that touch pitch will be defiled*: Proverbial, from the
   Apocrypha, Ecclesiasticus 13:1.

73 *present*: Represent.

77 *statutes*: Laws. F has *Statues* here, which is probably a
   printer's error, but is often kept by editors as an appropriate coinage of Dogberry's.

82 *Ha, ah ha*: Presumably a cry of triumph over Verges,
   and not laughter.

91 *coil*: Bustle.

97 *Mass*: More usually 'by the mass' (but cf. IV.2.49), a
   common interjection.

98 *scab*: Quibbling on the meaning 'scoundrel'.

101 *pent-house*: Overhang. This might be a reference to the
    canopy which projected over part of the stage in
    theatres like the Globe.

102 *drunkard*: See the note on I.3.37. Borachio refers, too,
    to the common proverb '*in vino veritas*', or, a man in

drink tells the truth.

105 *stand close*: Keep quiet and out of sight.

110 *be so rich*: Pay so much.

114 *unconfirmed*: Inexperienced.

116 *is nothing to a man*: Is nothing in respect of a man. Borachio means 'tells us nothing about a man', but Conrade takes the phrase in the sense 'is of no consequence to a man'.

121 *thief*: Used in a general sense to mean 'rogue'.

127–34 *Seest thou not . . . as his club*: Borachio's images are wild and eccentric, reflecting his character rather than actual fashions, though these were notoriously extravagant; see III.2.30 and note.

130–31 *Pharaoh's soldiers in the reechy painting*: This was probably a picture of the drowning of Pharaoh's soldiers in the Red Sea when they were pursuing Moses (Exodus 14:23–8).
       reechy: Filthy.

131 *god Bel's priests*: Alluding to the story of Bel and the dragon in the Apocrypha.

132–4 *shaven Hercules . . . codpiece seems as massy as his club*: This may perhaps be an allusion again to the story of Omphale (see II.1.232–3 and note), but it seems to be confused with the tale of Samson and Delilah in Judges 16:17–19.
       codpiece: Pouch, sometimes conspicuous and ornamented, at the front of breeches worn by men. This Hercules was depicted in the costume of Shakespeare's age.

141 *leans me out*: The use of *me* is here emphatic, drawing attention to the speaker, and 'is equivalent to "mark me", "I tell you"' (E. Abbott, *A Shakespearian Grammar* (1879), § 220).

145 *possessed*: Instructed.

155 *temple*: Church.

160 *right*: A term of respect, as in 'right honourable'.

164 *lock*: Lovelock, or hanging curl, which was fashionable among some men of the age.

169–70 *Never speak . . . go with us*: This sentence is assigned to Conrade in Q and F, where it seems certain that a

speech-prefix for the Watchman was inadvertently
omitted.

171–2 *goodly commodity . . . these men's bills*: Very useful,
being arrested on the strength of these men's halberds.
But there is also a quibbling allusion to fine goods
obtained on credit (*taken up*) in exchange for bonds
(*bills*).

173 *in question*: Meaning both 'subject to legal examination'
and 'of doubtful value'.

III.4

It is now the following morning, five o'clock as Beatrice
tells us at 46, and the characters are dressing for the
wedding. Much of the fun of this scene is generated
in the way Margaret rouses the interest of Beatrice,
almost reveals the plot of III.1 and then cleverly diverts
her suspicion.

6 *rebato*: Stiff ornamental collar.

12 *tire*: Decorative head-dress.
within: It is not seen onstage.

16 *exceeds*: Is most superior.

17 *nightgown*: Dressing-gown, often finely made of silk or
satin and faced with fur. See II.3.134 and note.

18 *cuts*: Made in the edge of a garment for ornament, and
to show a contrasting colour underneath.

19 *down-sleeves, side-sleeves*: The first were full-length
fitted sleeves, the second loose, open sleeves hanging
from the shoulder for ornament.

20 *underborne*: Trimmed underneath. This could refer to
a petticoat displayed beneath the dress or to a trim-
ming along and inside the edge of the skirts to stiffen
them.
tinsel: Fabric interwoven with gold or silver thread.
quaint: Elegant.

26–7 *Is not marriage honourable in a beggar*: The allusion is
to Hebrews 13:4: 'Marriage is honourable among all'
(Geneva Bible (1587)).

29 *saving your reverence*: A phrase of apology introducing
a remark that might offend. Hero's prudishness,
Margaret suggests, would have found the word

'husband' more acceptable than 'man'.

29, 32 *an*: If.

33 *light*: Playing on the sense 'wanton'.

37 *tune*: Mood.

39 *Clap's into*: Let's strike up.
   'Light o'love': This was a popular tune; several ballads were set to it but the original words seem to be lost. Shakespeare plays on the title also in *The Two Gentlemen of Verona*, I.2.83.

40 *burden*: Bass accompaniment, or, as Margaret means, a man.

41 *Ye light o'love, with your heels*: Beatrice suggests that Margaret will lie down (be 'light' or wanton) with any man; 'light-heeled' meant 'unchaste'.

43 *barnes*: Both 'barns' and 'bairns' or babies.

44 *illegitimate*: Playing on the meanings 'unwarranted' and 'born out of wedlock'.

47–8 *heigh-ho! . . . a husband*: *heigh-ho!* might be a cry used in hawking or riding, or a sigh for a husband. See II.1.295 and note.

49 *H*: Playing on 'ache' (pronounced 'aitch').

50–51 *an you be not turned Turk . . . sailing by the star*: To turn Turk is to change completely (cf. *Hamlet*, III.2.284–5). Margaret is saying that if the trick has not made Beatrice change her nature completely (by becoming a lover), the Pole Star can no longer be relied upon as a guide to navigation.

52 *trow*: I wonder.

53–4 *God send everyone their heart's desire*: See Psalm 37:4: 'Delight thou also in God: and he shall give thee thy heart's desire.'

55 *are*: Have.

57 *stuffed*: With a cold in the head, but Margaret takes it in a bawdy sense.

61 *professed apprehension*: Laid claim to wit.

66–7 *Carduus Benedictus*: The 'Blessed Thistle' (a herb much used medicinally).

68 *qualm*: Sudden sickness.

71 *moral*: Hidden meaning.

72–83 *Moral? . . . other women do*: Margaret talks nonsense to divert Beatrice's suspicion.

75 *list*: Please.

81 *eats his meat without grudging*: Is content.

82 *converted*: See II.3.21.

85 *false gallop*: Properly a canter, but Margaret quibbles, meaning 'I speak truth'.

III.5

This follows immediately on from the last scene; Dogberry and Verges apparently stay Leonato as he is hurrying to the wedding.

0 *Headborough*: This is the title of a parish officer with functions similar to those of the Constable but with more limited authority.

3 *decerns*: For 'concerns'.

11–12 *honest as the skin between his brows*: A common proverb, perhaps explained by another: 'Everyone's fault is written in his forehead.'

15 *palabras*: Be brief (properly *'pocas palabras'* – Spanish for 'few words' – a common phrase of the time).

20 *as tedious as a king*: Dogberry thinks *tedious* means 'rich' and distorts the proverb 'as rich as a king'.

21 *of*: On.

24 *exclamation on*: Literally, complaint or outcry against. Dogberry again picks the wrong word.

29 *excepting*: For 'respecting'.

30 *arrant knaves*: Downright rogues.

33 *When the age is in, the wit is out*: Garbling the proverb 'when ale is in, wit is out'.

33–4 *it is a world*: It is a great thing, a marvel (a proverbial phrase).

35 *God's a good man*: Proverbial phrase, meaning 'God is good'.

35–8 *an two men ride of a horse . . . all men are not alike*: These are more proverbial phrases; Dogberry's speech is a tissue of common sayings.

39 *he comes too short of you*: Leonato means in size, not in sense; Dogberry is to be imagined as a big man and Verges as slender.

43 *aspicious*: Confusing 'suspicious' with 'auspicious'.

47 *suffigance*: For 'sufficient'.

52–3 *Francis Seacoal*: Presumably the same as George Seacoal; see III.3.11. Shakespeare is often inconsistent in unimportant details.

57 *that*: His brain. He points to his head.

   non-come: Perhaps he means to say 'nonplus', but in fact suggests '*non compos mentis*', that is, he will drive them out of their minds.

IV.1

1–3 *plain form . . . particular duties*: To speed the action, the Friar is made to omit the preamble in the service on the responsibilities of marriage.

10 *inward*: Secret.

19–20 *Interjections . . . ah, ha, he*: Benedick jestingly alludes to the section on interjections in William Lily's Latin grammar (1549, and often reprinted), the standard school grammar, which Shakespeare knew well, and cites several times in his plays.

21 *Stand thee by*: Stand aside.

   by your leave: If I may so call you.

28 *learn*: Teach.

35 *that blood as modest evidence*: That blush as evidence of modesty.

36 *witness*: Bear witness to.

39 *luxurious*: Lustful.

42 *approvèd*: Established.

43 *proof*: Trial, attempt.

46 *known*: Had intercourse with.

47–8 *embrace me as a husband . . . the 'forehand sin*: A marriage by pre-contract, or the formal and witnessed acceptance of each other by a man and a woman, was legally valid, and so they might reasonably have embraced 'beforehand'.

50 *large*: Free or immodest.

55 *Dian*: Diana, goddess of the moon, and of chastity.

57 *blood*: Sensual appetite.

60 *wide*: Mistakenly (wide of the mark).

63 *stale*: Prostitute.

72 *kindly*: Natural (as belonging to a father).

80 *Hero itself*: That is, the very name, if it becomes a byword for lust; he heard Borachio call Margaret 'Hero'. Through the story of Hero and Leander, in which she drowns herself for love, Hero became a type of faithfulness, and Shakespeare may have had this in mind.

85 *then are you no maiden*: By denying what they know for a fact, she confesses her guilt.

87 *grievèd*: Wronged.

90 *liberal*: Licentious.

97 *much misgovernment*: Flagrant misconduct.

104 *conjecture*: Evil suspicion.

109 *Come, let us go*: Don John hustles away his dupes; things have worked out as he wished and it would serve no purpose for Claudio to stay longer.

110 *spirits*: Vital powers.

120 *printed in her blood*: Shown in her blushes, and stamped on her life.

124 *on the rearward of reproaches*: Immediately after reproaching you.

126 *frame*: Scheme of things, plan. Capulet complains similarly over his daughter in *Romeo and Juliet*, III.5.164–7.

134 *mine and mine I loved and mine I praised*: Each *mine* refers to his daughter, the *she* of 137.

136–7 *That I myself . . . Valuing of her*: In caring so much for her, I had no thought or regard for myself.

138 *that*: Such that.

140–41 *season give | To*: Make sound again (literally, give relish to).

155 *given way unto this course of fortune*: Allowed matters to go on in this way.

156 *By noting of*: Because I have been carefully watching.

160–61 *a fire . . . burn the errors*: An image derived from the burning of heretics in religion at the stake.

164 *experimental seal*: The test of experience.

164–5 *warrant | The tenor of my book*: Confirm the substance of my reading.

173 *proper*: True.

180 *unmeet*: Improper.

181 *change*: Exchange.

182 *Refuse*: Spurn.

183 *misprision*: Mistake.

184 *very bent of*: A complete devotion to. The phrase origi-
   nated as a metaphor from archery; see II.3.218 and note.

186 *practice*: Treacherous contriving.

187 *in frame of*: In plotting.

192 *invention*: Power to scheme, inventiveness. The word
   is pronounced here as four syllables.

195 *kind*: Manner.

196 *policy of mind*: Practical wisdom.

198 *quit me of them throughly*: Settle accounts thoroughly
   with them.

200 *Princes left for dead*: Q and F both have *Princesse* (*left
   for dead*) but Hero is no princess, whereas Don Pedro,
   and perhaps Don John, who left her *for dead*, may both
   properly be called princes.

201 *in*: At home.

203 *mourning ostentation*: Formal show of mourning.

209 *remorse*: Sorrow.

216 *to the worth*: At its proper value.

218 *rack*: Exaggerate (stretch as on the rack of torture).

223 *study of imagination*: Introspective broodings (cf. the
   phrase 'brown study').

224 *organ of her life*: Feature of her living body.

225 *habit*: Dress.

226 *moving*: Both 'full of motion' and 'affecting'.

229 *liver*: Regarded as the seat of love and the passions.

232 *success*: What follows (not distinguished in early usage
   as good or bad).

233 *event*: Outcome.

235 *if all aim but this be levelled false*: If we miss our aim
   in every other respect except this (referring to *suppo-
   sition* in the next line).

238 *sort*: Turn out.

240 *reclusive*: Cloistered.

243 *inwardness*: Friendly attachment.

247 *Being that I flow in grief*: Since I overflow, or am overwhelmed by, grief; *flow* also suggests easy movement,
and so Leonato can be pulled along by a thread.

250 *to strange sores . . . strain the cure*: Variant of the common
proverb 'A desperate disease must have a desperate
cure'.

252 *prolonged*: Postponed.

261 *even*: Direct.

263 *office*: Task.

266 *As strange as the thing I know not*: Beatrice seems to be
about to confess her love, but ends cautiously. The rest
of her speech is mere equivocation.

271 *eat it*: Eat the words of your oath, deny it.

275–6 *protest*: Swear.

279 *in a happy hour*: At a propitious moment.

289 *I am gone though I am here*: I have gone in spirit, though
I am held here by force.

297 *approved*: Confirmed.

299 *bear her in hand*: Delude her with false pretences.

301 *uncovered*: Barefaced.

310 *counties*: Counts (see II.1.328).

311 *count*: Quibbling on 'count' meaning each particular
charge in an indictment.
Count Comfect: Sugar-plum count, a title pouring further
derision on Claudio.

314 *curtsies*: Ceremony. The word applied to an obeisance
made by either sex.

315 *only turned into tongue*: Turned into voices only.
trim: Glib.

315–17 *He is now as valiant as Hercules . . . swears it*: Mere
words nowadays suffice to establish a reputation for
valour, and no one asks for deeds.

IV.2

Dogberry and Verges now examine their prisoners, as
Leonato instructed them to do at III.5.45. This presumably takes place at about the same time as the wedding
and no time interval is to be imagined.

0 *Sexton*: Q has *Towne clearke*, that is, the parish clerk,
evidently the same person as the Sexton, who was earlier

named as Francis Seacoal (see III.5.52–3).

0 *gowns*: A black gown was the official dress of a constable, and of a sexton.

2 *stool and a cushion*: So that he can sit and write notes. He should be carrying his *pen and inkhorn* (III.5.53).

5 *exhibition*: For 'commission'.

12 *sirrah*: A contemptuous form of address, hence Conrade's reply. Dogberry is by turns familiar and domineering with the accused.

19 *defend*: Forbid.

26 *go about with*: Get the better of.

30–31 *both in a tale*: That is, they say the same thing. Dogberry is amazed to find them in agreement in answering a question he has just put to both of them.

34 *eftest*: Quickest. This is Dogberry's invention, perhaps a corruption of 'deftest'.

49 *by mass*: Properly 'by the mass', a common oath.

65 *opinioned*: Pinioned.

66–71 *VERGES Let them be – in the hands ... CONRADE Away! You are an ass*: Some confusion arose in the printing of this passage in Q; 66–7, *Let them be in the hands of Coxcombe*, are assigned as one speech to *Couley*, or Richard Cowley, the actor in Shakespeare's company who played Verges. The compositor, perhaps confusing the abbreviations 'Cou' (Cowley) and 'Con' (Conrade), must have run two speeches together. The arrangement of the text here makes the best dramatic sense, for clearly Conrade should call Dogberry *coxcomb*.

66 *be – in the hands*: Let their hands be bound.

68 *God's my life*: Abbreviating 'God save my life', a common exclamation.

70 *naughty*: Wicked.

81–2 *a fellow that hath had losses*: He boasts that he is rich now, but once was even richer.

82 *two gowns*: Clothes were expensive and Dogberry's claim to own two gowns, or cloaks trimmed with fur or velvet, establishes his modest affluence.

V.1

7 *suit with*: Match.

12 *answer every strain for strain*: Correspond, pang for pang.
    strain also suggests the meaning 'tune', as *answer* could
    mean to sing antiphonally.

16 *sorry wag*: Pitiful jester. This is the best emendation of
    sorrow, wagge, (Q and F), which makes nonsense.
    cry 'hem!': In hesitation or doubt.

17–18 *make misfortune drunk | With candle-wasters*: Drown
    sorrow in philosophy.
    candle-wasters: Bookworms, burners of midnight oil.

24 *preceptial medicine*: Medicine composed of precepts.

27 *office*: Business.

28 *wring*: Writhe.

29 *sufficiency*: Ability.

30 *moral*: Full of moral precepts.

32 *advertisement*: Advice.

33 *Therein do men from children nothing differ*: In other
    words, you are being childish.

37 *writ the style of gods*: Affected a god-like superiority in
    their writings.

38 *made a push at chance and sufferance*: Scoffed at misfor-
    tune and suffering.

46 *Good-e'en*: Good evening (properly, God give you good
    even, a greeting used at any time after midday).

49 *all is one*: No matter for that.

55 *beshrew*: A curse on.

57 *to*: In moving to.

58 *fleer*: Gibe.

62 *to thy head*: To your face.

66 *trial of a man*: To fight – a judicial trial by combat.

72 *My villainy*: Claudio seems not to notice the news of
    Hero's death and burial, but is concerned only for himself.

75 *nice fence*: Skill at fencing.

78 *daff me*: Brush me off.

80–101 *He shall kill two of us . . . me deal in this*: Antonio, now
    so angry, has just been preaching patience to Leonato.

82 *Win me and wear me*: Proverbial phrase, meaning 'let
    him overcome me, and he is welcome to boast'.

84 *foining*: Thrusting (a fencing term).

91 *apes*: Fools.

91 *Jacks*: Knaves (see I.1.171 and note).

93 *utmost scruple*: Last ounce (an apothecary's measure equalling 20 grains, a tiny amount).

94 *Scambling*: Scuffling.

fashion-monging: Constantly changing fashions.

95 *cog*: Cheat.

flout: Mock.

96 *anticly*: Grotesquely.

show outward hideousness: Have a frightening appearance.

102 *wake your patience*: Urge you to forbearance.

115 *with*: By.

117 *doubt*: Incline to think.

122 *high-proof*: Proved in the highest degree.

127–8 *bid thee draw, as we do the minstrels*: Claudio does not realize that Benedick is serious.

128 *draw*: A musical instrument from its case.

131–2 *care killed a cat*: A common proverb.

133 *in the career*: At full charge (an image from tilting with lances at tournaments).

133, 169, 199 *an*: If.

136 *broke cross*: Snapped in the middle (a mark of clumsiness in the tilter, who was supposed to carry his lance straight against his opponent, and not swerve aside, when it might be broken).

139 *he knows how to turn his girdle*: He knows he must put up with it, for no one will mind him. The reference is to a common proverb: 'If you be angry, you may turn the buckle of your girdle behind you.'

144 *Do me right*: Give me satisfaction.

protest: Proclaim.

149–50 *calf's head and a capon*: By imputation, Claudio abuses Benedick as a fool (*calf*) and a weakling.

151 *curiously*: Skilfully.

152 *woodcock*: Simpleton (from the ease with which this bird was taken in a snare).

159 *wise gentleman*: Ironically suggesting a fool or wiseacre.

160 *hath the tongues*: Knows several languages.

164 *trans-shape*: Transform.

165 *properest*: Most handsome.

171 *old man's daughter*: Meaning Hero and referring to III.1.

172–3 *God saw him . . . in the garden*: Alluding to Genesis 3:8, where Adam tries to hide from God.

174–7 *savage bull's horns . . . married man*: See I.1.242–7, where Benedick boasted he would never submit to the yoke as the *savage bull* does.

179 *gossip-like*: Tattling.

192 *pretty*: Fine (in an ironic sense).

192–3 *goes in his doublet and hose . . . his wit*: Goes ready to fight, and puts aside his intelligence. A man would prepare for action by taking off his cloak, which suggested Don Pedro's jest.

194–5 *He is then a giant to an ape . . . doctor to such a man*: He then seems to a fool (*ape*) to be a hero; but a fool is then wise compared to such a man.

195 *doctor*: Man of learning.

196 *pluck up*: Rouse yourself.

197 *sad*: Serious.

199 *reasons*: Quibbling on 'raisins'; the words were much closer in pronunciation than they are now; see *Henry IV, Part I*, II.4.235)

203 *Hearken after*: Enquire into.

215 *well suited*: Nicely set out. He means that Don Pedro has found four ways of saying the same thing.

218 *cunning*: Clever.

238 *Sweet Hero*: Only now, on hearing of Hero's innocence, does Claudio's love revive; the Friar had expected that the news of her death would do the trick; see IV.1.212–34.

239 *rare semblance that*: Fine or lovely likeness in which.

258 *patience*: Pronounced as three syllables.

260 *Impose*: Subject.

268 *Possess*: Inform.

270 *invention*: Poetic skill, imagination (pronounced as four syllables).

271–2 *Hang her an epitaph . . . sing it tonight*: This was suggested by the Friar at IV.1.203–6.

275 *daughter*: Invented for the occasion; at I.2.1–2 it was mentioned that Antonio has a son.

278 *right*: Quibbling on 'rite': either way the phrase means 'make her your wife'.

284 *naughty*: Wicked.

286 *packed*: Involved as an accomplice.

291–2 *under white and black*: In writing.

294–5 *one Deformed*: Dogberry embroiders on what was over-heard at III.3.121–4.

304 *God save the foundation*: Dogberry gives thanks as if he had received alms at some religious foundation.

317 *lewd*: Base.

V.2

6 *style*: Quibbling on 'stile'.

7 *come over*: Surpass, and cross.

9 *come over me*: A sexual quibble. An undercurrent of bawdy allusion runs through the jesting of this scene, especially the dialogue with Margaret.

10 *keep below stairs*: Remain a servant (and not become a 'mistress').

17 *bucklers*: Small shields used for warding off thrusts. Benedick says, in effect, 'I surrender'.

21 *pikes*: The spikes which were mounted in the centre of bucklers.
    vice: Screw. Benedick's bawdy jest is plain enough.

26–9 *The God of love ... I deserve*: These lines, printed as prose in Q and F, were the beginning of an old song, now lost, but referred to often enough to suggest that it was well known.

30–31 *Leander ... Troilus ... panders*: These are stock examples of legendary faithful lovers. Leander's swimming of the Hellespont to visit Hero was celebrated in Christopher Marlowe's *Hero and Leander* (1598); Troilus used Pandarus as his go-between in wooing Cressida.

32 *quondam carpet-mongers*: Former ladies' men. A carpet-monger was one who frequented boudoirs or private and carpeted rooms.

37 *innocent*: Silly.

45 *came*: Came for.

54 *subscribe him*: Write him down. Benedick refers here to his challenge at V.1.142–5.

57–8 *so politic a state*: Such a well-organized rule.

61 *epithet*: Expression.

68–70 *praise himself . . . good neighbours*: They are quibbling over the common proverb 'he who praises himself has ill neighbours'. Benedick claims that good neighbours no longer exist and so men must praise themselves.

74 *Question*: Roughly equivalent to 'since you ask me, I'll answer'.

75 *rheum*: Tears.

76 *Don Worm, his conscience*: Probably alluding to the common image of conscience as a tormenting *Worm* or serpent; see Isaiah 66:24 and Mark 9:44.

87 *old coil*: Great confusion.

88 *abused*: Deceived.

90 *presently*: At once.

92–3 *die in thy lap and be buried in thy eyes*: The image of sexual orgasm as dying was common in lyric poetry of the period; see Shakespeare's Sonnet 92, l.12.

V.3

This scene needs to recapture the solemn ceremonial of the marriage scene, IV.1. The *monument* here displayed is referred to in that scene by the Friar as *your family's old monument* (204). This night scene marks the passage of time to a new day (25–7).

0 *tapers*: Wax candles for devotional use.

3 *CLAUDIO . . . Epitaph*: Q and F simply print the heading *Epitaph*; and do not assign it to a speaker; they provide a speech-prefix for Claudio at 11, *Now, music, sound*.

5 *guerdon*: Recompense.

11 *Song*: Q and F name no singer of the Song; it is best assigned to Balthasar, who was the singer at II.3.60.

12–13 *goddess of the night . . . slew thy virgin knight*: Diana, the moon goddess, imaged as an armed huntress, was patroness of virgins, who might be called her *knights*.

20 *utterèd*: Expressed, commemorated.

26 *wheels of Phoebus*: Wheels of the sun god's chariot.

30 *weeds*: Clothes. They are wearing black cloaks or some

costume suggesting mourning.

32 *Hymen now with luckier issue speed's*: May the god of marriage prosper us with a happier outcome.

V.4

6 *question*: Investigation.

7 *sort*: Turn out.

14 *office*: Function.

17 *confirmed*: Composed. The word was accented on the first syllable.

20 *undo*: Quibbling on the sense 'ruin'.

30 *marriage*: Pronounced as three syllables.

34 *assembly*: Pronounced as four syllables; cf. *tickling*, III.1.80.

41 *February face*: Benedick is still showing his disapproval of Don Pedro and Claudio.

43–51 *savage bull . . . just his bleat*: See I.1.241–7 and V.1.174–7; Claudio expands the earlier jesting in this allusion to the story of Jupiter changing himself into a bull in order to carry off the maid Europa. He also implies that Benedick will be a glorious cuckold (*we'll tip thy horns with gold*), and Benedick retorts in kind.

52 *I owe you*: I'll pay you back.

54, 56 *ANTONIO*: Leo(nato) in Q and F, but see 15–17 above.

67 *qualify*: Moderate.

69 *largely*: Fully.

71 *presently*: At once.

83 *but in friendly recompense*: Except as a return of friendship.

87 *halting*: Limping.

97 *Peace! I will stop your mouth*: Wrongly assigned to Leonato in Q and F.

101–3 *if a man will be beaten with brains . . . nothing handsome about him*: If a man goes in fear of witticisms, he will not dare to wear finery – much less, he implies, will he dare to marry.

105 *flout*: Mock.

112 *double-dealer*: Both a married man and an unfaithful husband.

119 *of*: On.
121–2 *There is no staff . . . tipped with horn*: This alludes once
more to cuckolds' horns. The *staff* is *reverend* both as
the emblem of the prince's authority, and as the badge
of old age.

The National: three theatres and so much more…
www.nationaltheatre.org.uk

In its three theatres on London's South Bank, the National presents an eclectic mix of new plays and classics, with seven or eight shows in repertory at any one time.

And there's more. Step inside and enjoy free exhibitions, backstage tours, talks and readings, a great theatre bookshop and plenty of places to eat and drink.

Sign-up as an e-member at www.nationaltheatre.org.uk/join and we'll keep you up-to-date with everything that's going on.

NATIONAL THEATRE
SOUTH BANK
LONDON SE1 9PX

PENGUIN SHAKESPEARE

ALL'S WELL THAT ENDS WELL
WILLIAM SHAKESPEARE

WWW.PENGUINSHAKESPEARE.COM

A poor physician's daughter cures the King of France, and in return is promised the hand of any nobleman she wishes. But the man she chooses, the proud young Count of Rosillion, refuses to consummate the forced marriage and flees to Florence. Depicting the triumph of trickery over youthful arrogance, *All's Well that Ends Well* is among Shakespeare's darkest romantic comedies, yet it remains a powerful tribute to the strength of love.

This book includes a general introduction to Shakespeare's life and the Elizabethan theatre, a separate introduction to *All's Well That Ends Well*, a chronology of his works, suggestions for further reading, an essay discussing performance options on both stage and screen, and a commentary.

Edited by Barbara Everett

With an introduction by Janette Dillon

General Editor: Stanley Wells

Penguin Shakespeare

AS YOU LIKE IT
WILLIAM SHAKESPEARE

WWW.PENGUINSHAKESPEARE.COM

When Rosalind is banished by her uncle, who has usurped her father's throne, she flees to the Forest of Arden where her exiled father holds court. There, dressed as a boy to avoid discovery, she encounters the man she loves – now a fellow exile – and resolves to remain in disguise to test his feelings for her. A gloriously sunny comedy, *As You Like It* is an exuberant combination of concealed identities and verbal jousting, reconciliations and multiple weddings.

This book includes a general introduction to Shakespeare's life and the Elizabethan theatre, a separate introduction to *As You Like It*, a chronology of his works, suggestions for further reading, an essay discussing performance options on both stage and screen, and a commentary.

Edited by H. J. Oliver

With an introduction by Katherine Duncan-Jones

General Editor: Stanley Wells

PENGUIN SHAKESPEARE

CYMBELINE
WILLIAM SHAKESPEARE

WWW.PENGUINSHAKESPEARE.COM

The King of Britain, enraged by his daughter's disobedience in
marrying against his wishes, banishes his new son-in-law. Having fled
to Rome, the exiled husband makes a foolish wager with a villain he
encounters there – gambling on the fidelity of his abandoned wife.
Combining courtly menace and horror, comedy and melodrama,
Cymbeline is a moving depiction of two young lovers driven apart by
deceit and self-doubt.

This book includes a general introduction to Shakespeare's life and the
Elizabethan theatre, a separate introduction to *Cymbeline*, a chronology
of his works, suggestions for further reading, an essay discussing
performance options on both stage and screen, and a commentary.

Edited with an introduction by John Pitcher

General Editor: Stanley Wells

PENGUIN SHAKESPEARE

MEASURE FOR MEASURE
WILLIAM SHAKESPEARE

WWW.PENGUINSHAKESPEARE.COM

In the Duke's absence from Vienna, his strict deputy Angelo revives an ancient law forbidding sex outside marriage. The young Claudio, whose fiancée is pregnant, is condemned to death by the law. His sister Isabella, soon to become a nun, pleads with Lord Angelo for her brother's life. But her purity so excites Angelo that he offers her a monstrous bargain – he will save Claudio if Isabella will visit him that night.

This book includes a general introduction to Shakespeare's life and the Elizabethan theatre, a separate introduction to *Measure for Measure*, a chronology of his works, suggestions for further reading, an essay discussing performance options on both stage and screen by Nicholas Arnold, and a commentary.

Edited by J. M. Nosworthy

With an introduction by Julia Briggs

General Editor: Stanley Wells

PENGUIN SHAKESPEARE

A MIDSUMMER NIGHT'S DREAM
WILLIAM SHAKESPEARE

WWW.PENGUINSHAKESPEARE.COM

A young woman flees Athens with her lover, only to be pursued by her would-be husband and by her best friend. Unwittingly, all four find themselves in an enchanted forest where fairies and sprites soon take an interest in human affairs, dispensing magical love potions and casting mischievous spells. In this dazzling comedy, confusion ends in harmony, as love is transformed, misplaced, and – ultimately – restored.

This book includes a general introduction to Shakespeare's life and the Elizabethan theatre, a separate introduction to *A Midsummer Night's Dream*, a chronology of his works, suggestions for further reading, an essay discussing performance options on both stage and screen, and a commentary.

Edited by Stanley Wells

With an introduction by Helen Hackett

General Editor: Stanley Wells

read more ⓟ

PENGUIN SHAKESPEARE

ROMEO AND JULIET
WILLIAM SHAKESPEARE

WWW.PENGUINSHAKESPEARE.COM

A young man and woman meet by chance and fall instantly in love. But their families are bitter enemies, and in order to be together the two lovers must be prepared to risk everything. Set in a city torn apart by feuds and gang warfare, *Romeo and Juliet* is a dazzling combination of passion and hatred, bawdy comedy and high tragedy.

This book includes a general introduction to Shakespeare's life and the Elizabethan theatre, a separate introduction to *Romeo and Juliet*, a chronology of his works, suggestions for further reading, an essay discussing performance options on both stage and screen, and a commentary.

Edited by T. J. B. Spencer

With an introduction by Adrian Poole

General Editor: Stanley Wells

PENGUIN SHAKESPEARE

TWELFTH NIGHT
WILLIAM SHAKESPEARE

WWW.PENGUINSHAKESPEARE.COM

Separated from her twin brother Sebastian after a shipwreck, Viola disguises herself as a boy to serve the Duke of Illyria. Wooing a countess on his behalf, she is stunned to find herself the object of his beloved's affections. With the arrival of Viola's brother, and a trick played upon the countess's steward, confusion reigns in this romantic comedy of mistaken identity.

This book includes a general introduction to Shakespeare's life and the Elizabethan theatre, a separate introduction to *Twelfth Night*, a chronology of his works, suggestions for further reading, an essay discussing performance options on both stage and screen, and a commentary.

Edited by M. M. Mahood

With an introduction by Michael Dobson

General Editor: Stanley Wells

PENGUIN SHAKESPEARE

THE TWO GENTLEMEN OF VERONA
WILLIAM SHAKESPEARE

WWW.PENGUINSHAKESPEARE.COM

Leaving behind both home and beloved, a young man travels to Milan to meet his closest friend. Once there, however, he falls in love with his friend's new sweetheart and resolves to seduce her. Love-crazed and desperate, he is soon moved to commit cynical acts of betrayal. And comic scenes involving a servant and his dog enhance the play's exploration of how passion can prove more powerful than even the strongest loyalty owed to a friend.

This book includes a general introduction to Shakespeare's life and the Elizabethan theatre, a separate introduction to *The Two Gentlemen of Verona*, a chronology of his works, suggestions for further reading, an essay discussing performance options on both stage and screen, and a commentary.

Edited by Norman Sanders

With an introduction by Russell Jackson

General Editor: Stanley Wells

PENGUIN SHAKESPEARE

THE WINTER'S TALE
WILLIAM SHAKESPEARE

WWW.PENGUINSHAKESPEARE.COM

The jealous King of Sicily becomes convinced that his wife is carrying the child of his best friend. Imprisoned and put on trial, the Queen collapses when the King refuses to accept the divine confirmation of her innocence. The child is abandoned to die on the coast of Bohemia. But when she is found and raised by a shepherd, it seems redemption may be possible.

This book includes a general introduction to Shakespeare's life and the Elizabethan theatre, a separate introduction to *The Winter's Tale*, a chronology of his works, suggestions for further reading, an essay discussing performance options on both stage and screen by Paul Edmondson, and a commentary.

Edited by Ernest Schanzer

With an introduction by Russ McDonald

General Editor: Stanley Wells

Read more in Penguin

PENGUIN SHAKESPEARE